C000192613

The A to Z of Football

Written by **Michael Heatley**

THE A TO Z OF FOOTBALL

This edition first published in the UK in 2009
By Green Umbrella Publishing

© Green Umbrella Publishing 2009

www.gupublishing.co.uk

Publishers Jules Gammond and Vanessa Gardner

All rights reserved. No part of this work may be reproduced or utilised in any form or by any means, electronic or mechanical, including photocopying, recording or by any information storage and retrieval system, without prior written permission of the publisher.

Printed and bound in Italy

ISBN: 978-1-906635-25-1

The views in this book are those of the author but they are general views only and readers are urged to consult the relevant and qualified specialist for individual advice in particular situations.

Green Umbrella Publishing hereby exclude all liability to the extent permitted by law of any errors or omissions in this book and for any loss, damage or expense (whether direct or indirect) suffered by a third party relying on any information contained in this book.

All our best endeavours have been made to secure copyright clearance for every photograph used but in the event of any copyright owner being overlooked please address correspondence to Green Umbrella Publishing The Old Bakehouse, 21 The Street, Lydiard Millicent, Swindon SN5 3LU

Contents

AC Milan

▶ The AC Milan team celebrate after their 2007 Champions League success over Liverpool.

The Senior of the two Milan clubs (Inter, with whom they share the San Siro Stadium, split from them in 1908), AC was founded in 1899 by a group of expatriate Englishmen seemingly as keen on playing cricket as football. By winning their first Italian league title two years later, the club nailed its sporting colours to the mast and further success followed.

Milan were in the vanguard of importing foreign players, Swedes Gunnar Gren, Gunnar Nordahl and Nils Liedholm proving effective in the Fifties. The club's name was first engraved on a European trophy in 1963 after a star-studded team beat Benfica to claim the European Cup; managed by tactical genius Nereo Rocco, it included two future managerial legends in Giovanni Trapattoni and Cesare Maldini, with Gianni Rivera the midfield playmaker and Brazilian Jose Altafini the goalscorer. The Scudetto and Cup Winners' Cup in 1968 were followed by a second European Cup win, 4-1 over Ajax, with Rivera voted European Player of the Year.

Having hit an all-time low in 1980 with demotion from Serie A due to financial irregularities, the club was restored to its former glory by media magnate and future Italian Prime Minister Silvio Berlusconi. His appointment of Arrigo Sacchi accompanied by investment in such superstar names as the Dutch international triumvirate of van Basten, Gullit and Rijkaard led to great success in the late Eighties. Cesare Maldini's son Paolo was a defensive stalwart and is still at the club as captain despite being in his forties.

Sacchi's successor Fabio Capello continued the success, four Serie A titles in five years between 1992-96 setting the standard for others to follow. Victory over Barcelona in the 1994 European Champions League was particularly sweet, but they lost at the final hurdle the following year. 2003 saw them claim the ultimate European club title for the sixth time, and they

followed this with their 17th Scudetto in 2004. More recently, Milan were involved in the 2006 Serie A scandal where five teams were accused of fixing matches by selecting favourable referees. Milan were initially punished with a 15 point deduction and consequently did not qualify for the Champions League. An appeal saw their penalty reduced to eight points and they were allowed to retain their 2006-07 Champions League participation, where they won the competition under manager Carlo Ancelotti.

Ajax

▼ Ajax legend Johan Cruyff seen here in 1969.

The reputation of Amsterdam's premier club, Ajax, is based as much on their reputation for nurturing young talent (first established under long-serving coach Jack Reynolds between 1915 and 1949) as the achievements of its senior team. Neeskens, Haan, Cruyff and Krol in the Seventies were followed by Rijkaard, Bergkamp and van Basten who, in their turn were succeeded by Kluivert, Overmars and Seedorf.

The first quartet mentioned helped Ajax win the European Cup, predecessor of the Champions League, for three successive seasons from 1971, and also formed the backbone of Holland's World Cup final team in 1974. Counting domestic titles and the World Club Cup, Ajax held a "nap hand" of five titles in 1972, a feat unlikely ever to be beaten. Their success was built on "total football", a free-flowing style promoted by coach Rinus Michels allowing the players the tactical freedom to move away from rigid positional play.

Cruyff, who captained club and country, returned as coach in the mid Eighties to win the European Cup Winners' Cup in 1987, while a successful UEFA Cup campaign in 1992 made Ajax only the second club ever to have won the three major European competitions.

Louis van Gaal guided Ajax to the European Champions League title in 1995, where they beat AC Milan 1-0, but the break-up of that winning team underlined the fact that Ajax have always been a selling club. The advent of the Bosman ruling saw the likes of Reiziger, Davids, Frank and Ronald De Boer leave the Dutch capital for fame and fortune elsewhere.

Ajax's move the following year from the De Meer Stadium into the sixth home in their history – the magnificent Amsterdam Arena, with its 55,000 seats – still failed to stop the flow of their biggest names leaving such as winger Ryan Babel to Liverpool and playmaker Wesley Sneijder to Real Madrid.

The club founded in 1900 by a group of Amsterdam businessmen who met for kickabouts on a Sunday had come a long way. Yet their top priority, to re-establish themselves as a major European force, has yet to be realised but with their former star striker Marco van Basten (who formerly managed the national team at Euro 2008) at the helm, there is renewed hope.

▲ Rafael van der Vaart of Ajax and Holland is tackled by Claude Makelele of France during their international friendly in March 2004.

Arsenal

Founded in 1886, Arsenal were known originally as Woolwich Reds, later as Woolwich Arsenal, and eventually simply as Arsenal. The Gunners have been in the top division of the league since 1919 although, as any Tottenham supporter will tell you, they should by rights have begun the first season after the First World War in Division Two. They finished fifth in the old Division Two in 1915, but were mysteriously elected to Division One when league football recommenced after the cessation of hostilities. For many years afterwards, the team was labelled "Lucky Arsenal".

The Thirties was, until recently at least, the heyday of Arsenal Football Club. They were League Champions in 1931, 1933, 1934, 1935 and 1938 – a record run of five consecutive Championships being thwarted by Everton in 1932. Arsenal were runners-up that year. Their success was due in no small part to their legendary manager, Herbert Chapman, who had guided Huddersfield to similar success a decade earlier. The Gunners continued to be a major force after the Second World

War, and have frequently featured in European competition since the late Sixties. Ten years after Tottenham Hotspur did the League and FA Cup Double in 1961, their North London neighbours did it themselves – and went on to repeat the achievement in 1998 and 2002. The traditional rivalry between the sides still exists, but in recent times the Gunners have definitely had the upper hand. This has largely been due to manager Arsene Wenger who arrived at Highbury in September 1996 and has the rare ability to bring in young and unknown players – such as Thierry Henry, Cesc Fabregas, Emmanuel Adebayor and Theo Walcott – and turn them into superstars.

The Premier League and Cup were secured in 2004 (with the team unbeaten in the league) and 2005 respectively, and Arsenal also reached the Champions League final in 2006 which they narrowly lost to Barcelona. The club moved down the road to the 60,000-capacity Emirates stadium in July 2006 but have yet to repeat the success they were enjoying at Highbury. Most observers feel it is only a matter of time before glories return with Wenger's latest crop of wonderkids.

◀ Herbert Chapman, hero of the Thirties.

◀◀ Manager Arsene Wenger unveiling Theo Walcott who became the youngest player ever to represent England.

▼ Success for Arsenal under Arsene Wenger.

Beckham

▶ LA Galaxy's David Beckham with the ball during a tour match against South China at the Hong Kong Stadium on March 9th, 2008.

▶▶ Wayne Rooney of England celebrates with David Beckham as he scores their fourth goal during a 2010 World Cup qualifying match.

David Beckham is arguably the most famous footballer in the world. Blessed with model looks and married to Victoria, a former Spice Girl, he makes headlines both on and off the pitch.

But it is to his eternal credit that the glamour-life has rarely interfered with his football since he first signed for Manchester United as a trainee in January 1993. He helped the club win the Premier League in 1996 and 1997 and the FA Cup in 1996 and the following year was named PFA Young Footballer of the Year.

By then he had already broken into the England side on a regular basis and was part of the side that took the country to the World Cup finals in France in 1998. His World Cup experience was not exactly as had been planned, as he was dismissed against

Argentina for an innocuous tackle and England went out of the tournament.

The following few months saw him the subject of verbal abuse from spectators around the country, but "Becks" had the ability to override such criticism and within the space of two years he had become the fans' favourite, not least for his ability to weigh in with vital goals, especially in the crucial World Cup qualifier against Greece in 2001. He exorcised the Argentinean ghost with the only goal of the game from the penalty spot in England's second group match in Japan, a goal that went some considerable way towards removing Argentina from the competition.

Having helped United to six league titles, two FA Cups and the European Champions League, he was surprisingly deemed surplus to requirements at Old Trafford and sold to Real Madrid for £25 million in the summer of 2003.

In the World Cup qualifier against Poland in 2005, David became the first England player to have been sent off twice, earning his marching orders after two yellow card offences. He resigned as England captain after the 2006 World Cup finals and was dropped from the team by new coach Steve McClaren.

In January 2007, he agreed a deal worth a reported £250 million to join LA Galaxy and despite joining this football backwater earned a surprise recall to the England team winning his 100th cap and continuing to be picked by England manager Fabio Capello, his old coach at Real Madrid.

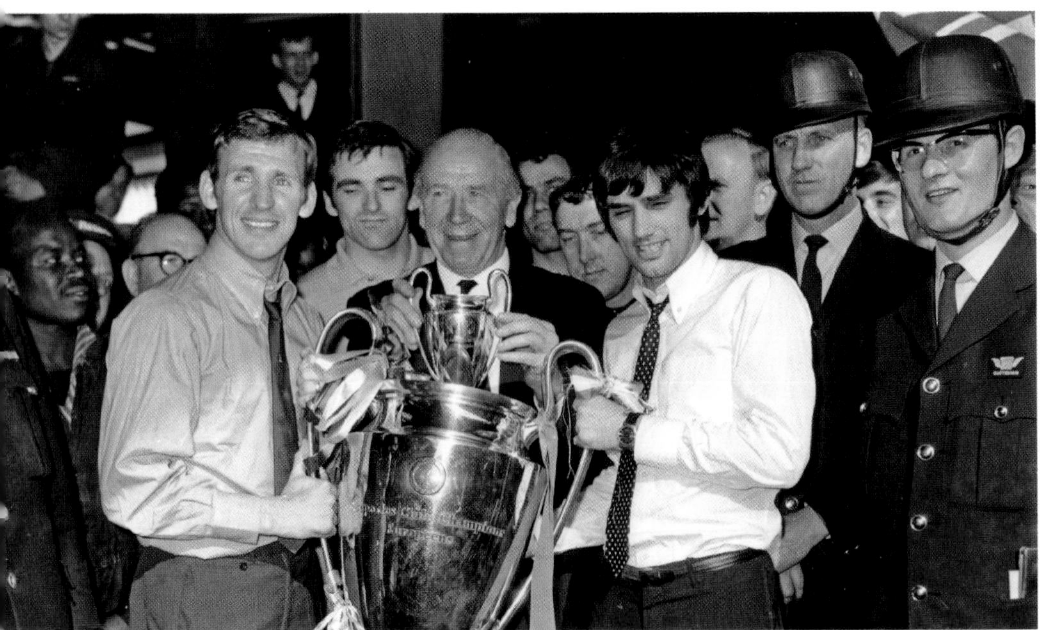

▲ George Best with Pat Crerand and Sir Matt Busby holding the European Cup, 1968.

Best

George Best is a football legend. Born in Belfast on 22nd May 1946, the young winger came to Old Trafford as a 15-year-old. Manager Matt Busby put him into the Manchester United first team in September 1963 and he soon became one of the greatest players the world had ever seen.

Best went on to score 178 goals in 466 United appearances. He was young, glamorous and fashionable and he had the world, as well as the ball, at his feet. A European Cup winner in 1968, his lightning speed and superb ball control meant that he was soon to be called up by Northern Ireland and, for a few short years, there was no-one to touch him. In the end, however, it all became too much. Idolised by millions, Best pursued a lifestyle that attracted a great deal of adverse publicity and his game, as well as his health, began to go into decline.

George Best in the Sixties was probably more popular than David Beckham is today but, unlike Beckham, Best seemed doomed to self-destruction. Problems with women, problems with alcohol and problems with turning up for games eventually led to his quitting United in 1973. He was still only 27 but, even though he later made 42 league appearances for Fulham and also played in the United States, his career was effectively over. His international career was also over, after just 37 games for Northern Ireland.

Best, dubbed "El Beatle" by the foreign press, was the first footballer to become part of the pop star/celebrity culture, and it did him no favours. When his playing days were finally over, he made a living through guest appearances and television punditry. He died in November 2005, aged 59, losing a long battle with illnesses linked to alcoholism, and his death was mourned worldwide.

▲ The funeral cortege for George Best.

Brooking

▼ Trevor Brooking playing for West Ham.

Trevor Brooking spent 18 years as a professional at West Ham United, his only senior club, a remarkable length of time given that many of his peers were regularly moving between clubs.

After being spotted playing schools and representative football for Ilford, Essex and London, Brooking was taken on as an apprentice by West Ham in July 1965 and was upgraded the following year.

He went on to make 528 league appearances for the Hammers, scoring 88 goals and helped the club win the FA Cup in 1975 and 1980, scoring the only goal of the game in the latter final against Arsenal. His goal was made all the more special by the fact it was a header; only the third headed goal of his career!

Brooking also appeared in the final of the European Cup Winners' Cup in 1976, the League Cup final in 1981 and won a Second Division Championship medal in 1981.

Having represented England at schoolboy, Youth and Under-23 level he was awarded his first full cap in 1974 and remained a regular until the 1982 World Cup, appearing as a substitute in the last match against Spain as England drew 0-0 and went out of the competition – England lost only seven of the 47 games he appeared in.

He retired as a player in May 1984 but has twice stepped into the breach as caretaker manager at his beloved West Ham. Having previously been made an MBE for his service to football Brooking was awarded the CBE in the 1999 New Year's Honours List and was later knighted for his services to football. In December 2003, he joined the FA as director of football development.

Champions League

The European Champions League came into being in season 1992-93 as a result of the two-leg knockout European Cup competition (founded in 1955) being reorganised into a hybrid league and knockout format. This had the benefit of guaranteeing those teams who qualified more than two games in the spotlight (and the accompanying financial rewards via television, etc), but the title of the competition was devalued in many eyes when clubs other than domestic champions were admitted.

The number of clubs that could be entered by any country and their entry point in the competition (there are three preliminary rounds) depended on the national association's position in UEFA's rankings. In a further dubious move, the third-placed teams knocked out in the group stages had the consolation of deferred entry into the UEFA Cup; Arsenal in 2000 and Celtic in 2003 both reached the final of that competition after qualifying through the "back door".

But the Champions League goes

▼ Liverpool captain Steven Gerrard and defender Jamie Carragher lift the European Cup after beating AC Milan, 2005.

▼ The slip by John Terry that cost Chelsea the match, 2008.

from strength to strength, fuelled by media hype and television money. Marseille were the first winners in 1993, though victory was tainted by corruption allegations. Ajax's win two years later unwittingly showed the peculiarity of the system as they beat AC Milan twice in their group and a third time in the final. Since then, Real Madrid have been the dominant force, notching three victories in the new format to go with six in the old European Cup (five of these coming in its first five years).

British clubs, were free to participate in the new competition, having been re-admitted into Europe in 1991 after the Heysel tragedy, but it wasn't until 1999 that Manchester United engraved a UK name on the trophy – the third leg of a famous Treble including the Premier League and FA Cup being achieved by two last-gasp goals from Sheringham and Solskjaer against Bayern Munich.

Unlikely as it seemed, Manchester United's late, late show of 1999 was eclipsed in 2005 by Liverpool, who reversed a 3-0 first half deficit against AC Milan to win the match on penalties after extra time. Having finished fifth, they then mounted a campaign to ensure the holders would be able to defend the trophy irrespective of domestic league position.

Arsenal came close to winning in 2006 when they lost by the odd goal to Barcelona, as did Chelsea in 2008 when a slip by skipper John Terry in the penalty shootout meant that the Cup went to Manchester United instead who completed the Double having also won the Premier League that year.

Charltons

Nobody really expected the Charlton brothers, who were nephews of the legendary Newcastle centre-forward Jackie Milburn, to both play for England. Jack Charlton, born in Ashington, Northumberland in 1935, began and ended his career with Leeds United, making 628 league appearances and scoring 70 goals, but he did not make it into the England side until he was almost 30. Over the years he did, however, become a very efficient centre-half, but was playing mainly in the old Second Division and at first no-one took much notice. "The Giraffe" as the lanky Jack was known, seemed doomed to remain in the shadow of his younger brother Bobby who, two and a half years his junior, was becoming a star forward with Manchester United.

Bobby was different. In all, he was to make more than 750 appearances for United, and score 198 goals in 606 league games. He came to prominence after the Munich air disaster, in which many of his Manchester United colleagues were killed, and he went on to play in a remarkable 106 internationals, scoring a record 49 goals. One of these games was the 4-2 victory over West Germany in the 1966 World Cup final, by which time his brother had joined him in the side.

▲ Jack (top row, fourth from right) and Bobby Charlton (front row, right) pose with the 1966 World Cup winning team.

Jack played 35 times for England. When his playing career was over, he went into management, taking the reins first at Middlesbrough, then at Sheffield Wednesday and then, for just over a year, at Newcastle United. In 1986 he took over the Republic of Ireland side and led his players to unprecedented success. In 1988, Ireland reached the European

▲ Bobby and Jack Charlton relaxing on the day before the World Cup final, 1966.

Championship finals, where they beat England 1-0, and two years later Jack guided them to the last eight in the World Cup finals.

It often happens that fairly ordinary players make successful managers and that great players enjoy less success in the field of management. While no-one would suggest that Jack Charlton was an ordinary player, it is true that he was a far more successful manager than his brother. Bobby became manager of Preston North End in 1973, but his side was relegated to the Third Division in 1974 and Charlton resigned a little over a year later. He stayed in the game, running a football school and becoming a director of Manchester United, but he will always be remembered for his fierce shot, his pace and his amazing body swerve – oh, and that trademark "comb-over" hairstyle.

Chelsea

Chelsea may now be one of the big four teams in the country but for most of its 100-year history it has not been so. Founded in 1905, the club had only a solitary League Championship in 1955 and a smattering of cups to show for their efforts before the Russian revolution took place.

Based a stone's throw from the King's Road, the "Blues" have always been a trendy team particularly in the early 1970s when such flamboyant players as Peter Osgood and Charlie Cooke helped them win the FA Cup over Leeds and Cup Winners' Cup against Real Madrid. But the following decades were turbulent times and the club was rescued from ruin by larger-than-life chairman Ken Bates in the early 1990s. It was not until the appointment of former European Footballer of the Year Ruud Gullit as player-manager in 1996 that their fortunes started to change.

He added several top-class international players to the side, particularly Gianfranco Zola, as the club won the FA Cup in 1997 and established themselves as one of England's top sides. Gullit was replaced by Gianluca Vialli who led the team to victory in the League Cup and the Cup Winners' Cup in 1998, the FA Cup in 2000 and the UEFA Champions League quarter-finals in 2000. Vialli was sacked in favour of another Italian, Claudio Ranieri, who guided Chelsea to the 2002 FA Cup final and Champions League qualification in 2002–03.

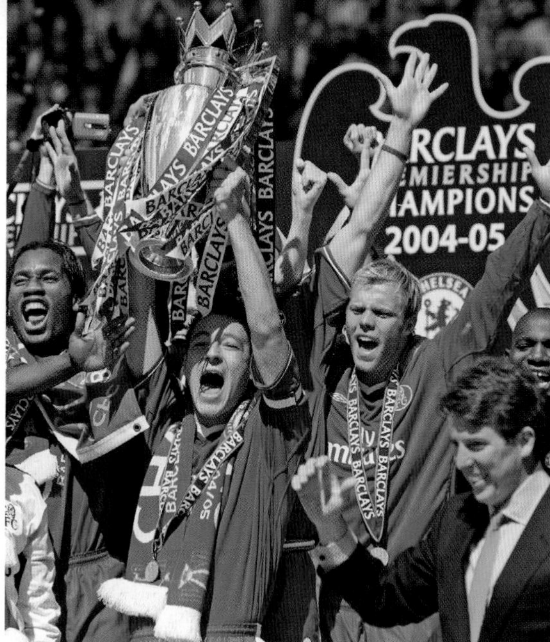

▲ John Terry celebrates with Chelsea players on lifting the Premier League trophy for the first time in 50 years.

In June 2003, Bates sold Chelsea to Russian billionaire Roman Abramovich for £140 million, completing what was

▲ Luiz Felipe Scolari directing his team.

then the biggest-ever sale of an English football club. Owing to Abramovich's Russian heritage, the club were soon popularly dubbed "Chelski" in the British media. More than £100 million was spent on new players, but Ranieri was unable to deliver any trophies, so he was replaced by successful Portuguese coach José Mourinho who had just guided Porto to victory in the UEFA Champions League.

In 2005, Chelsea's centenary year, the club became Premier League champions in a record-breaking season (most clean sheets, fewest goals conceded, most victories, most points earned), League Cup winners with a 3-2 win over Liverpool at the Millennium Stadium and reached the Champions League semi-finals. The following year, they were again League Champions, equalling their own Premier League record of 29 wins set the previous season. They also became the fifth team to win back-to-back Championships since the Second World War and the first London club to do so since Arsenal in 1933-34. In 2007, Chelsea won the FA Cup and League Cup, but finished runners-up to Manchester United in the Premier League.

After several disagreements with the owners, Mourinho parted company with Chelsea in September 2007 and was replaced by Israeli director of football Avram Grant, under whom the club finished as runners-up in the Premier League and the League Cup, and reached their first UEFA Champions League final, where they lost on penalties to Manchester United in May 2008.

Later that month, Grant's contract was terminated and former World Cup winning manager Luiz Felipe Scolari took over as manager bringing in yet more world class players such as Deco and former Blues legend Ray "Butch" Wilkins as assistant first team manager.

Derbies

Almost as soon as the new season's fixtures are published, fans across the country will quickly scan down their lists to see when they will be playing their nearest rivals. It is a custom that will be repeated in Bristol, Glasgow, Manchester, Liverpool, North London and Birmingham and everywhere in-between; the two fixtures against your local rivals will be the most eagerly awaited games of the season.

Close rivalry does not just exist within the town or city boundaries. Derby and Nottingham, Sunderland and Newcastle, Stoke and Port Vale and even down the league at Swansea and Cardiff or Darlington and Hartlepool, the clashes between two close rivals are guaranteed to raise most interest. There is more than just three points or progress into the next round of the Cup at stake; invariably the winners will invoke bragging rights for the next couple of months, making the lives of their rival-supporting workmates, friends or even families hell until revenge can be gained.

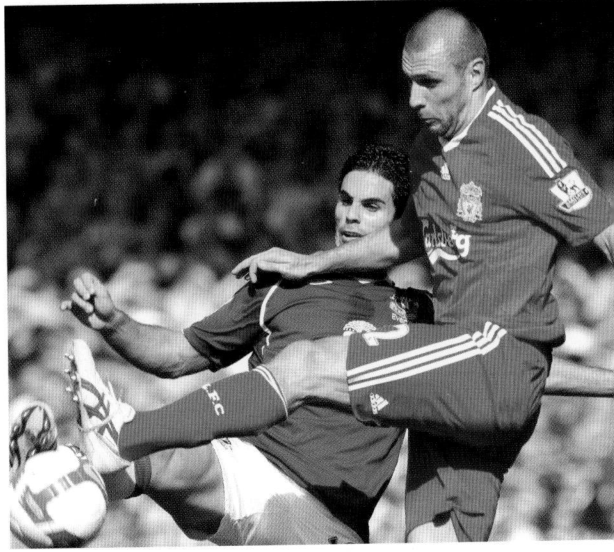

▲ Mikel Arteta tackles Andrea Dossena during a 2008 derby.

In some cases, the rivalry between two clubs only exists off the pitch; there are countless stories of Spurs and Arsenal players living next door and giving each other a cheery wave as they make their respective ways to training! Similarly, Liverpool owe their existence to the fact that Everton, the original tenants

▲ Tempers flare between Newcastle and Sunderland, 2007.

of Anfield, upped sticks and moved across Stanley Park in protest at their rent being put up, the landlord forming Liverpool FC in their place!

In times of trouble, you can usually rely on your neighbour to help you out. Spurs shared Arsenal's ground during the First World War and the roles were reversed during the Second. Manchester United played at Maine Road whilst their ground was being rebuilt after bomb damage during the Second World War, and relationships between Everton and Liverpool were so cordial that the two clubs shared one programme for a time!

The rivalries may be intense, but there are always moments when they can be put in their place. That greatest of all managers, Bill Shankly, produced one of the greatest put-downs of all time, and they even chuckle about it at Goodison – according to Shankly, when Everton lined up to meet dignitaries at the 1966 FA Cup final, 12 months after Liverpool had lifted the Cup, the captain was asked where Everton was. "In Liverpool, Ma'am." "Of course," replied the Royal. "We had your first team here last year!"

▲ Preston North End were famously the first winners of the Double.

Double Winners

The abandonment of the European Cup Winners' Cup may have robbed the FA Cup of some of its magic, but it will be remembered, especially at Preston North End, Aston Villa, Tottenham Hotspur, Arsenal, Liverpool and Manchester United, that the FA Cup remains one half of the most sought-after Double in the domestic game.

Preston North End were the first to achieve the feat, back in 1888-89, the first season of the Football League, at the end of the season when they won the league without losing a match and the Cup without conceding a goal; not for nothing were they known as the Old Invincibles. Aston Villa repeated their success in 1897, winning the title by 11 points and the Cup with a 3-2 win over Everton.

Since so many sides had come close

▲ Manchester United celebrate their Champions League victory over Chelsea in 2008.

during the next 60 years only to fall at the final hurdle, there were many who believed the feat to be beyond a modern side. In 1958 Danny Blanchflower, the Irish and Spurs captain, could talk of little else, although over the next two years it appeared Wolverhampton Wanderers would be the next to achieve the feat, especially after winning the league title two years on the trot.

Spurs' exceptional start to the 1960-61 season (they won their first 11 matches and were unbeaten in 16) had them down as potential champions right from the off. By the time January came, Spurs were virtually out of sight in the league and could turn their attentions to the Cup. They were not at their best in the final against Leicester, but the 2-0 win allowed them to complete the first

Double of the modern era.

The fourth Double took another 10 years to achieve, this time by North London rivals Arsenal. Whilst they have lacked the flair of the Spurs side of 1961, there is no doubting their resourcefulness, tenacity and work-rate, factors that enabled them to overhaul Leeds United in the league (winning the league title by beating Spurs 1-0 at White Hart Lane in the final match of the season) and see off Liverpool in the Cup final.

It was Liverpool who next lifted both major domestic trophies in one season, something of a personal triumph for player-manager Kenny Dalglish, who scored the crucial goal in the league match at Chelsea to secure the title. It will not be forgotten inside Goodison Park, for Liverpool's Double in 1986 denied their city rivals Everton their own Double. As well as finishing runners-up in the league they were on the losing side in the Cup final, well beaten 3-1 on the day.

The arrival of the Premier League in 1992 may have changed the design of one of the trophies on offer but did not diminish the importance and relevance of the Double. Manchester United managed it twice in three years and might have made it three; Double winners in 1994 and 1996, they were runners-up in both competitions in 1995.

It was Arsenal's turn again in 1998, knocking Manchester United down to second place in the league and easily overcoming Newcastle United in the FA Cup final. Arsenal repeated the feat in 2002, as they continued to battle for domestic dominance with Manchester United.

The league title and FA Cup might be the ultimate domestic feat but it is starting to pale when compared to winning the Premier League and the Champions League.

Manchester United achieved this in 1999 and more recently in 2008 when they narrowly pipped Chelsea to the league as well as beating them on penalties in the final of the Champions League in a rainy May night in Moscow.

Such is the strength of the top teams in the Premier League that they now have their sights firmly set on winning this deluxe version of the Double at the start of every season, leaving mid-table sides such as Portsmouth to win the FA Cup!

Dribble

Jimmy Greaves scored many goals during his career, more than anyone else during the modern era. A large percentage of these were scored inside the six-yard box, an area Greaves was particularly familiar with, pouncing on a loose ball here, a dropped ball there to net yet another goal. For many fans, however, the greatest he ever scored in the white shirt of Spurs was his mazy run half the length of the field against Manchester United in 1965 when he rounded two or three defenders and the goalkeeper before slotting calmly home.

Whilst all about him was pandemonium, Jimmy Greaves acknowledged the goal with his customary single hand raised salute (like a 1960s Alan Shearer). Whilst Greaves might not have felt the goal special at the time he scored it, countless replays should by now have convinced even him that he scored something magical.

Think of all the great goals that have been scored during the history of the FA Cup. Whilst there will be one or two votes for Ronnie Radford's thunderbolt for Hereford against Newcastle United,

or Norman Whiteside's curled winner for Manchester United in the final of 1985 against Everton, the two most oft-shown goals remain Ricky Villa's winner in the final against Manchester City in 1981 and Ryan Giggs' extra time winner for Manchester United against Arsenal in 1999. Both involved a lot of dribbling, confusing the defence as the attacker turned first one way and then the other, never losing control of the ball or sight of the goal.

In Villa's case, the fact that the goal proved to be the winner lifted it to folklore status. In the case of Ryan Giggs' strike, keeping the Treble on track meant more to United's followers than either of the two winning goals in the final against Newcastle United. Outside United followers, who could instantly recall either?

The undoubted master of the dribble was Stanley Matthews. The whole of his career was built around his exceptional ball control, never better displayed than in the 1953 FA Cup final for Blackpool against Bolton. Blackpool scored three times in the final 20 minutes, Stan Mortensen completing a hat-trick, but it is Matthews' wizard dribbling to set up the win that has survived the passage of time.

The modern day master is Cristiano Ronaldo who has incorporated the step over into a fine art but still nonetheless mesmerises defenders with his silky skills and gets spectators up out of their seats.

◀ Cristiano Ronaldo showing his incredible dribbling skills.

▼ Ricky Villa with the ball at his feet.

England

England's status as the country that gave the world football has given her a privileged position as one of the top teams in the world, even if her results on the field have been significantly lower down the table.

It is this reputation that causes opposition to raise their game whenever they face England. England's position as the birthplace of the modern game has meant every foreign side wants to win at Wembley, more than any other venue in the world.

The long-redundant Home International Championships notwithstanding, a solitary World Cup win, achieved in 1966 at Wembley (and if England couldn't win it in their own backyard, where could they?) is not much to show for 140 years of endeavour. England's isolationist stance through the first 50 or so years of the 20th century and enforced absence during the 1980s, coupled with blind pursuit of tactics the rest of the world abandoned long ago, always seems to leave the English playing catch-up. Football's elite still seem to have a healthy lead, if the World Cup clash between England and Brazil in 2002 was anything to go by, even if there are the occasional moments when the gap seems to narrow, as evidenced by the 5-1 victory over Germany en route to the 2002 finals and the 4-1 rout of Croatia in the 2010 World Cup campaign.

Part of the problem lies with achievement always falling well short

of expectation. England were expected to retain the 1970 World Cup but fell apart in the quarter-final against West Germany although, had Gordon Banks been well enough to play, they should have advanced to the semi-final at least. They were then expected to at least qualify for the finals in 1974 and 1978, but allowed the Poles and Italians respectively to ease them out.

After stuttering through qualification to the 1982 finals, they started impressively and got steadily worse, running out of steam in the crucial match against Spain. Their performance in 1986, when they were ragged to begin with and got better, finally beaten by a dubious handball goal from Maradona in the quarter-final, followed the same pattern, flattering to deceive. Indeed, about the only tournament in which England did better than expected was the 1990 World Cup in Italy, when they made the semi-finals but lost out on penalties to their nemesis Germany. After missing out in 1994, England have returned to the quarter-finals but no further in the last three tournaments.

To be fair, England probably had a team capable of winning the 2004 European Championships under the management of Sven Goran Eriksson and with Rooney unleashed on the international scene but again the national team went out on penalties.

Under the management of Steve McClaren England didn't even make the 2008 Championships but, of course, hope springs eternal with new boss Fabio Capello.

◀ England's finest hour, the World Cup win of 1966.

▼ Disappointment for England as they lose to Croatia in a Euro 2008 qualifier.

European Championships

▶ The Arsenal team celebrating after scoring the last penalty to win the FA Cup final against Manchester United, 2005.

▼ Henri Delaunay, European visionary.

Whilst most record books tend to show European competition began in 1955 with the launch of the European Champions Club Cup, there were plenty of earlier competitions that are worthy of note. However, it was Henri Delaunay, secretary of the French Football Federation that first put forward the idea of the European Championships in 1956 (hence the actual trophy is named after him). Invitations to the member countries were extended for the inaugural competition to commence in 1958, but interest was somewhat lacking, with all four British countries and West Germany among the most noticeable absentees.

The semi-finals and final were to be played in Paris in July 1960. Yugoslavia ousted the hosts 5-4 and the Russians beat Czechoslovakia 3-0 to book their place in the showdown. Although Yugoslavia took the lead, the Russians finally won after extra time 2-1 to become the first winners of the Henri Delaunay Cup.

The competition has grown in both size and stature since those early days, flourishing in spite of one or two problems along the way – Greece refused to play Albania in 1964 since the two countries were technically at war! The format of group matches was introduced in 1968, along with a new name, the UEFA European Football Championship (the trophy itself was retained), although to begin with the group winners progressed into a two-legged quarter-final.

The collapse of the communist countries in Eastern Europe swelled UEFA's membership ranks to 48 and a new format was devised for the 1996 competition. The top 16 qualifiers would now be placed into four groups of four (similar to the World Cup finals), with the top two teams progressing into the quarter-finals. This format has been retained ever since as the European Football Championship has blossomed from its uncertain beginnings into the second most important event on the international football calendar.

FA Cup

The FA Cup is widely regarded as being the world's finest domestic knockout competition. Some say it is less important than it once was – but try telling that to the fans, or indeed, to the players. It all began in 1872, when the competition was instituted for what were then amateur clubs. The first winners were The Wanderers, and they repeated their success in 1873. Next, Oxford University, and then the Royal Engineers held the trophy aloft, before The Wanderers did it again for three successive seasons.

As professionalism began to take a hold, The Wanderers wandered off into the sunset and in 1884 the first of the "modern" clubs – Blackburn Rovers – won the Cup. They also won it three years running. In its early days, the Cup final was played at a variety of locations, including The Oval but at last, in 1923,

▲ Celebrations for Portsmouth after winning the FA Cup final, May 2008.

it found a permanent home at the Empire Stadium, Wembley.

The Cup final remained synonymous with Wembley until 2001, when it moved on a temporary basis to the Millennium Stadium, Cardiff, returning in 2007 when the new Wembley Stadium was at last ready.

The FA Cup has always provided shock results but, in modern times, no team outside the top two divisions has won the trophy. However, Tottenham Hotspur did become the first non-League club to win it after the formation of the Football League, their success coming in 1901. Manchester United currently hold the record for the highest number of FA Cup wins, having lifted the trophy 11 times. Arsenal are one behind after beating them in 2005.

Ironically, United withdrew from the competition in 1999-2000 to pursue the World Club Championship in Rio de Janeiro, thus refusing to defend the trophy they had won the previous season as part of an historic Treble. Happily, the FA continue to value and protect the competition's prestige, and it is good to report that, unlike the League Cup, the trophy has never yet been allowed to take a sponsor's name directly.

The FA Cup has only been won by a non-English team once in its history, Cardiff City were the club to achieve this in 1927. Eighty-one years later, in 2008 they made it to the final only to lose to Portsmouth.

Ferguson

Gritty Glaswegian Alex Ferguson failed to make headlines in a playing career that spanned six clubs north of the border and peaked at Rangers between 1967-69, but found unparalleled success as a manager.

Starting at St Mirren in 1975, he broke the mould of Scottish football while manager of Aberdeen, winning three Championships, four Scottish Cups and the European Cup Winners' Cup in six years. Along with Dundee United, the Dons under Ferguson smashed the Old Firm (Celtic and Rangers)'s monopoly of honours. He joined Manchester United in 1986 as a somewhat dour successor to the flamboyant Ron Atkinson. His first three seasons brought little – chairman Martin Edwards resisting the call for Fergie's head after a 5-1 walloping by neighbours City in 1989 – but after the Red Devils took off again with an FA Cup win in 1990 they dominated the English domestic game in the way Liverpool dominated the late 1970s and 1980s.

Ferguson increasingly featured home-grown youngsters like David Beckham, Paul Scholes, Nicky Butt and the Neville brothers, Gary and Phil alongside the big-name buys, and these, along with David Beckham, would become England international regulars. United recorded two League and Cup Doubles, the first English club

▲ Sir Alex Ferguson applauds the fans as he heads for the dressing room.

▲ Sir Alex Ferguson, 2008.

ever to achieve the feat, and took four of the first five Premier Leagues, but critics claimed the retirement of Eric Cantona would bring an end to the glory days. Fergie and his Fledglings (the new Busby Babes) proved the doubters wrong as in 1999 they swept all before them en route to an historic Treble of Premier League, FA Cup and European Cup. A knighthood was the wily Scot's reward as his team carved a unique place in the record books with their clean sweep of domestic and European honours.

Ferguson's premature (and rescinded) decision to retire at the end of 2001-02 led to morale problems that season as Arsenal overtook them, while his personality clash with David Beckham arguably weakened the team sufficiently to ensure they could not retain the Premier League title in season 2003-04.

He quickly put these blips behind him and with his astute recruitment of players – Ferdinand, Rooney and Ronaldo to name but a few – has put Manchester firmly back on top of both English and European football.

He pioneered Premier League wins in 2006-07 and 2007-08 (the club now holds 10 Premier League titles) and an amazing Champions League victory in May 2008 when they emerged victorious over Chelsea on penalties.

As he approaches retirement, he can now be considered to be one of the greatest football managers in the history of the game, certainly in the history of English football. With 21 years under his belt, he is the second-longest serving manager in the history of Manchester United after Sir Matt Busby, and the longest serving current manager in English football, having won a slew of awards and holding many records including winning Manager of the Year most times in British football history.

Floodlights

The Football League did not approve the use of floodlights until the mid 1950s, but the first English football match to be played under them took place at Bramall Lane, Sheffield in 1878. Dynamos were used to power the lights, which were attached to wooden towers.

Floodlights meant that games could be played at any time during the dark winter days. There were however many problems with reliability, and floodlighting failed to really take off until after the First World War. Even then, the Football Association was not keen on the idea, and it tried to prevent clubs from using them. After the Second World War, the pressure from clubs increased, and the FA gave way.

The first league club to install lights was Third Division (South) Swindon Town. They switched on their illuminations for a friendly in 1951, and many of the bigger clubs soon copied them. A few FA Cup games were subsequently played under lights, but the first Football League game to be floodlit took place in 1956, when Portsmouth entertained Newcastle.

▲ Floodlights at Charlton's Valley ground.

Within a few years only a couple of First Division grounds were without floodlights. The lights were mainly mounted on towers, one at each corner of the ground, and many of these towers survive to this day. Tower lighting does however tend to illuminate much of the surrounding area, often to the annoyance of local residents, and in more recent years there has been a move towards lighting along the edges of stand roofs. Floodlighting is today a very sophisticated science.

Gerrard

Steven Gerrard is for many the best midfield player in the country – usually winning the fans' vote as to whether he or Frank Lampard should play in the England side. It is generally accepted that they can't play together which is somewhat ironic as it has been Chelsea, for whom Lampard plays, who have regularly courted his services. He has stayed loyal to his local club Liverpool after breaking into the first team in 1998 and scored his 100th goal in a European tie in October 2008 with a trademark piledriver.

Scouser "Stevie G" became a vital part of the Liverpool side that won a unique Treble in 2001 of the League Cup, FA Cup and UEFA Cup and he also finished the season by winning the PFA Young Player of the Year Award. He eventually became Liverpool captain and guided them to further success in the League Cup in 2003 and two years later the ultimate prize, the UEFA Champions League. Indeed, it was this match that best epitomised Gerrard's worth to his club, for with Liverpool

3-0 down at half-time, he scored the vital first goal and was instrumental in their historic comeback.

He was awarded an MBE in the 2007 New Year's Honours List and in August 2008, he became Liverpool's most capped England player of all time after winning his 68th cap against the Czech Republic at Wembley. Some would argue that he has never played as well for his country as he has for his club but recent England managers all want him in their team as he always brings energy and commitment to the side.

◀◀ Steven Gerrard vying for the ball in a match against the Czech Republic, August 2008.

◀ Steven Gerrard in action against Bolton, 2008.

▲ Ian Porterfield's goal that gave Sunderland a shock win over Leeds.

Giantkillers

If there is one thing that encapsulates the magic of the FA Cup, it is giantkilling. When the draw is made, pitting some non-League or Third Division club at home to a Premier League club, interest is heightened by the prospect of a giantkilling.

It has always been this way. Arsenal may have one of the best records in the FA Cup, but in Walsall they will always remember the day back in 1933 when the Third Division side beat the League Champions 2-0 in the FA Cup third round. In fact, the result was such a shock that Arsenal manager Herbert Chapman singled out Tommy Black as the villain of the day, selling him to Plymouth Argyle within a week!

Whilst form and ability will even

out over the course of a league season, they often count for nothing in a one-off match. An unfamiliar pitch often plays its part, as Sunderland found to their cost in a cup tie at Yeovil in 1949 – although Sunderland took the lead, Yeovil's players were better equipped to cope with the sloping pitch and ran out 2-1 winners on the day. On other occasions, the elite cannot even use this as an excuse – Arsenal were held to a 2-2 draw at Highbury by Bedford in 1956 and Newcastle were held to a similar scoreline at home to Hereford in 1972.

The replays both ended 2-1, but whilst Arsenal managed to overcome their non-League opposition, Newcastle were on the receiving end of one of the biggest Cup upsets of all time, with Ronnie Radford netting a thunderbolt that has been shown on television prior to just about every round of the FA Cup ever since. As a result of their exploits, Hereford were subsequently voted into the league, as were Wimbledon as a result of victory over Burnley in 1975.

According to the form book, media and experts, the 1973 FA Cup final could only end in a Leeds United victory over Second Division Sunderland, but on the day goalkeeper Jim Montgomery played the game of his long and illustrious career and Ian Porterfield netted the only goal to register the biggest Cup final upset ever.

With the big clubs keen to reduce the number of matches they have to play, there's been talk of the FA Cup following its league counterpart and doing away with replays, all matches to be decided on the day. This would be sad, for what makes the FA Cup so magical is the regularity with which the underdog is able to upset his bigger rival.

▼ Giantkiller turned coach Jim Montgomery prepares Scarborough's keeper Leigh Walker to face Chelsea, 2004.

Giggs

If Ryan Giggs was born in the wrong generation, he has more than made his mark on football in general and Manchester United in particular. A throwback of some 20 or 30 years, his dazzling runs on the wing for United have created chance after chance for a grateful forward line for nearly 20 years.

Born in Cardiff on 29th November 1973, Giggs joined United straight from school and made his debut during the 1990-91 season. The following season he made 38 appearances and scored four goals as United battled with Leeds United for the league title, finally having to settle for runners-up spot. Compensation of sorts was reached in the Rumbelows Cup, with United beating Nottingham Forest 1-0 in the final to enable Giggs to collect his first winner's medal.

Since then he has become the most decorated player in the domestic game having won 10 Premier League titles with United and two Champions League trophies. Although he represented England at youth level, Giggs later opted to turn out for Wales

◀ Ryan Giggs limbering up before coming on as substitute in the Champions League final, 2008.

◀◀ Ryan Giggs lifts the Premier League trophy after helping his team beat Wigan, May 2008.

and went on to win more than 60 full caps for the country of his birth although he never played in a major international tournament.

Club records have continued to fall; on 20th February 2008 he made his 100th appearance in the UEFA Champions League in a game against Lyon, and on 11th May 2008 he came on as a substitute against Wigan to equal Sir Bobby Charlton's record of 758 appearances for United. Fittingly, Giggs scored the second goal in that match, sealing the league title for United and also marking the 10th time he has won the Premier League trophy. Ten days later, on May 21st 2008, Giggs broke Bobby Charlton's appearance record for United when coming on as an 87th minute substitute for Paul Scholes in the Champions League final against Chelsea. United would go on to win the final, defeating Chelsea 6-5 on penalties after a 1-1 draw after extra time. Giggs converted what became the winning penalty in sudden-death for United and joined Steve McManaman and team-mate Owen Hargreaves in becoming the only British players to have played in and won multiple Champions League finals.

Goals

It is not a sight seen on too many parks and fields these days, largely because most parks and fields already have goalposts erected, but not so long ago kids desperate for a game of football would grab anything to mark out a goal – the phrase "jumpers for goalposts" will invoke an instant reaction in anyone over 30!

As is fairly well known, football in England began as an inter-village game involving hundreds of players per side. There were no goals as such; the ball just got kicked and carried between two villages, up and down streams and rivers with no real target in sight.

Although the Football Association came into being in 1863, it was not until three years later that the FA refined the ruling on goalposts, passing the resolution that "the goals shall be upright posts, eight yards apart, with a tape across them, eight feet from the ground." This ruling remained in place for a further 11 years when, after consultation with the Sheffield FA and in a desire to get a uniform set of rules in place, the wording was amended to read "with a tape or bar across them, eight feet from the ground."

In 1889 J A Brodie of Liverpool patented goal nets, with a match in Bolton between two local sides on New Year's Day 1890 being the first occasion they were used. The next year was spent trying out the new invention, with the FA keen observers. Finally, in February 1891, the FA minutes reported,

"Mr J A Brodie was interviewed on the subject of his goal nets. The following resolution was carried; that the Council approve of the use of nets as under Mr Brodie's patent, but cannot

take any steps to amend the rule so as to make their use compulsory until some satisfactory arrangement can be made with the patents as to prices to be charged to clubs." Even now the use of nets is still optional.

In 1996 FIFA announced plans to make the goals wider by the diameter of two balls and taller by the diameter of one ball, agreeing to listen to opinion on the matter. Although the planned change would have taken place immediately after the 1998 World Cup, these plans were subsequently dropped.

No matter what size the goal is, or whether the nets are optional or compulsory, there is still a great feeling to be derived from scoring a goal, either in a town park or at Hampden Park. What a shame that those villagers of so many years ago never got to experience the thrill!

◀ A corner flag but no goalposts in sight in this early game of football.

▲ Geoff Hurst's controversial third goal in England's World Cup victory in 1966 did not hit the back on the net - but did it cross the line?

Half-Time

▲ A half-time pep talk.

Half-time is the period when managers can re-motivate teams, teacups can be thrown and substitutions planned. For the spectator, it's a chance to be fed and watered, which in practice often means joining the loo and/or burger-bar queue. The length of the interval seems to have increased from 10 to 15 minutes by stealth; a FIFA meeting in 2004 debated but then rejected a German motion to further increase this to 20 minutes, studies in that country having shown that a five-minute extension would mean an increase of at least £200,000 a year per club in food and drink takings.

Almost every ground in Britain features some form of timepiece to count down the 45-minute halves. These days, however, the time is usually displayed digitally. Half-time scoreboards appear, by and large, to be a thing of the past. Jumbo TV-style screens now offer not only scores but highlights of previous games, advertisements and messages. Half-time entertainment can include penalty shootouts, schoolboy games, dance troupes, club mascots or the traipsing around the pitch of a so-called legendary player.

Perhaps the biggest innovation, however, is the advent of half-time betting. When Manchester City came back from 3-0 down at Tottenham to win 4-3 in early 2004, a gambler – who wasn't even a City fan – won a reported six figure sum backing them to win the cup tie by that exact score. He certainly had a better outcome than the fan who left the ground...

◀ Bournemouth's James Hayter celebrates his "three in two" feat.

Hat-trick

A hat-trick in football is when a player scores three goals in a game and claims the match ball. The term is borrowed from cricket, where a new hat would be given to a bowler who claimed three wickets with consecutive balls. (Others claim that, in the days when footballers got the bus to the match with fans, the passing round of a hat to collect money was a way of rewarding a player for his on-field efforts.) Goals do not need to be scored consecutively, however, as with wickets in cricket.

Arguably the most famous hat-trick ever is the one Geoff Hurst scored for England at Wembley in the 1966 World Cup final to secure the trophy for the home nation. Though the first in a final, it was not the first to be scored in the final stages; that was by Guillermo Stabile of Argentina in their 6-3 win over Mexico in 1930. The first by a substitute was claimed by Laszlo Kiss of Hungary in a match against El Salvador in 1982. Last but not least, Gabriel Batistuta of Argentina became the only player to date to have scored a hat-trick in successive World Cup tournaments against Greece in 1994 and Jamaica four years later.

Returning to England, Spurs' Willie Hall entered the record books by scoring three goals in four minutes against Northern Ireland in a Home International Championship match in November 1938. England were 1-0 up before Hall's 36th, 38th and 40th minute first half goals. He scored twice more in the second half to notch up five of England's seven without reply.

Bournemouth striker James Hayter

▲ Theo Walcott scoring the first of three goals in the 2010 World Cup qualifying match against Croatia.

broke English records when he notched three goals in two minutes 20 seconds for Bournemouth against Wrexham in February 2004. This was all the more remarkable because he had come on as a second half substitute and scored his first with his first touch of the ball. His parents who live on the Isle of Wight had left Dean Court to catch the ferry, believing he was unlikely to feature in the match, and missed the action.

The Premier League record is held by Robbie Fowler, who notched a four minute 35 second treble for Liverpool against Arsenal in 1994.

The youngest ever player to score a hat-trick for England was Theo Walcott who notched his trio against Croatia in a World Cup qualifier in September 2008 at just 19 years of age.

Internationals

We have Charles Alcock, secretary of the FA between 1870 and 1896, to thank for the FA Cup and international matches. He proposed the former, based on the inter-house knockout competitions he had observed whilst at school at Harrow, in 1871, and the FA Cup has gone on to become perhaps the best known cup competition of all. He proposed the latter a year earlier, in 1870, and took part himself in the first, albeit unofficial match between England and Scotland that was played at Kennington Oval in March 1870 and ended all square at 1-1. There were to be a further four unofficial England and Scotland clashes, all played at Kennington Oval, although all of the players involved were based in London and Arthur Kinnaird (later Lord Kinnaird) turned out for Scotland in at least one of these clashes.

It was Alcock's desire to see Scottish players further afield interested in his proposal that led him to advertise for players in the *Glasgow Herald* in November 1870.

Although Queen's Park, the leading Scottish side of the day, read the letter with interest and sent former player Robert Smith as an observer, it was to take a further two years before England finally met Scotland in anything approaching an official capacity. Queen's Park entered the very first FA Cup competition, were exempt (on the grounds of travelling difficulties) until the semi-final and held Wanderers to a creditable draw. They were unable to afford to travel down again for the replay and therefore withdrew, but had in the meantime contacted Wanderers' secretary Charles William Alcock and suggested that they could organise a

proper England-Scotland fixture.

As the Scottish Football Association was not formed until 1873, Queen's Park were seen as the "establishment" in Scotland and their offer was eagerly taken up by Charles Alcock. Queen's Park offered to guarantee the expenses of the travelling England side, and so on 30th November 1872, at the West of Scotland Cricket Club at Hamilton Crescent, England and Scotland met in the very first international match.

The England-Scotland clash was the only international until 1879 when England met Wales for the first time and 1882 when they travelled to Belfast to meet Ireland. With regular fixtures in place, a British Championship was introduced in 1884 and survived for 88 seasons until it was abandoned in 1984. The success, however, of the competition was noted with interest overseas and in 1904 Belgium and France met at Uccle, near Brussels in the first international match ever to be played outside Great Britain.

Four years later England played their first overseas international matches. By the 1920s virtually every country had played an international match and interest in the game worldwide was such that there were calls for an international competition. By 1930 this became reality with the creation of the World Cup.

Ireland

The England and Ireland clash in Belfast in 1882 was Ireland's very first international match, but the rest of the day went downhill; Oliver Vaughton and Arthur Brown became the first English players to register hat-tricks (Vaughton ended the match with five goals, Brown four) as England won 13-0!

Despite this unfortunate start Ireland eagerly accepted an invitation to take part in the British International Championship when it was launched in 1884. To begin with the Irish made up the numbers; they didn't beat the Welsh until 1887, the Scottish until 1899 and had to wait until 1913 before they finally got the better of the English!

With the creation of the Republic of Ireland in 1926, it was Northern Ireland who continued to compete in

▲ Giovanni Trapattoni being unveiled as the new manager of the Republic of Ireland team.

◀ David Beckham receiving his 100th cap from Sir Bobby Charlton.

the British Championship. To all intents and purposes, the rest of the Home Countries ignored the Republic, at least football-wise, with England not playing them until 1946, Wales until 1960 and Scotland until 1961. Even more surprisingly, Northern Ireland and the Republic of Ireland have met in only one friendly international since 1926, in 1999, although they have been drawn in the same qualifying groups for either the European Championships or World Cup four times.

Whilst Northern Ireland's greatest moments on the world stage were in the 1958 and 1982 World Cups, when they qualified from the group stage, the Republic had to wait longer before making an impact. The appointment of former England international Jack Charlton galvanised the country and helped the Republic qualify for the 1990 World Cup finals in Italy.

Charlton worked a miracle again in getting the side to the finals of the European Championships in 1992 and the World Cup in 1994. His successor Mick McCarthy did equally well to qualify for the final tournament in Japan and Korea in 2002.

Ireland pulled off one of the greatest managerial coups of all time when they appointed Giovanni Trapattoni – the most successful manager ever in the history of European club competition – in 2007.

Italy

▲ Italy suffers World Cup humiliation in 1966 at the hands of North Korea.

◀ Ireland celebrating a World Cup penalty in 2002.

Founded in 1898, the Italian Football Association is one of Europe's oldest and, with three World Cup wins and a European Championship victory, one of its most successful. For the last 40 or so years, Italy has also been the home of some of the most successful European club sides, seeing Juventus and both Milan clubs, AC and Inter, triumph in the European Cup.

Hosts for the very first World Cup tournament played in Europe in 1934, the Italian side was somewhat hijacked by the political aspirations of dictator Benito Mussolini. If Italy were to stage the World Cup, then they had to win it.

Italy's passage to the final was not all plain sailing, having to overcome Greece in a qualifier and being involved in a violent clash with the Spaniards in the quarter-final that required a replay before Italy finally won 1-0. They fell behind in the final against Czechoslovakia, were forced to switch their forwards around in a desperate bid to get on terms and finally won the match in extra time.

Four years later Italy became the first side to successfully defend their world title. Although only two of the 1934 side retained their place in the 1938 team, a fair few had helped Italy win gold at the 1936 Olympic Games.

The outbreak of the Second World War brought international football to a standstill, but it is worth recording that for the duration of the war Ottorino Barassi, the secretary of the Italian FA, kept the Jules Rimet trophy in safe-keeping in a shoe box hidden under his bed!

Despite producing some enterprising sides after the war had ended, most notably Torino in the late 1940s, Italian football for the next 30 or so years became remembered for its negativity. Despite luring goalscorers of the calibre of Jimmy Greaves, Denis Law and later Ian Rush with the promise of huge salaries, Italian football was seldom exciting even if it was successful.

A disastrous World Cup in 1966, when they were eliminated in the group stages by North Korea (the Italian team were pelted with rotten fruit when they arrived home!) was followed by a better showing in 1970 in Mexico. After qualifying from their group with one victory, two draws and just a single goal, they opened up a little in the quarter-finals, beating the host nation 4-1.

▼ A dejected Italian team after they were knocked out of the UEFA European Championship.

Italy then played their part in one of the most thrilling World Cup matches of all time in overcoming the West Germans 4-3 in the semi-final, but in the final the mighty Brazilians ran out easy 4-1 victors.

Eliminated early on in 1974, Italy finished fourth in 1978 and were fortunate to qualify out of their group in 1982, drawing all three of their matches. Thereafter, Italy got better as

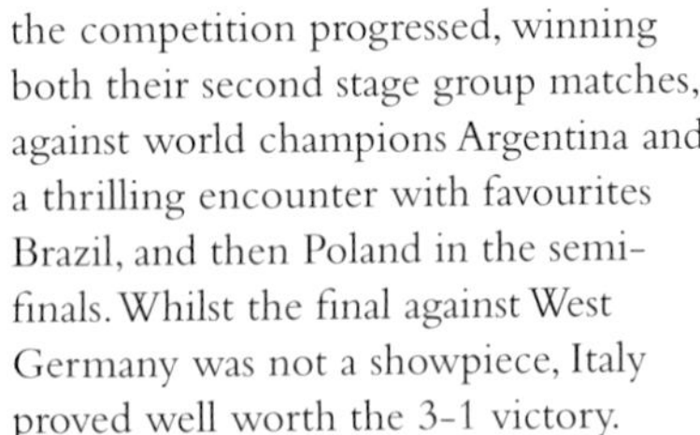

the competition progressed, winning both their second stage group matches, against world champions Argentina and a thrilling encounter with favourites Brazil, and then Poland in the semi-finals. Whilst the final against West Germany was not a showpiece, Italy proved well worth the 3-1 victory.

They reached the final again of the 1994 tournament in the US, where they were unfortunate to lose on penalties to the Brazilians. The Azzurri won their fourth World Cup, defeating their long-time rivals France in Germany in 2006 winning 5-3 on penalty kicks after a 1-1 draw at the end of extra time. They had been greatly helped by the sending off of French captain Zinedine Zidane after he head butted defender Materazzi but manager Marcello Lippi had assembled a very difficult team to beat even if they didn't play with typical Latin lavishness.

Lippi retired after the tournament and the team was taken into the 2008 European Championships by 1994 World Cup star Roberto Donadoni but he was dismissed after they were dourly knocked out by the eventual winners Spain. It was time to call again for Lippi to mastermind their challenge for the 2010 World Cup.

James

Taken on by Watford as a trainee in 1988 he spent four years at Vicarage Road, becoming recognised as one of the best goalkeepers outside the top division and regularly being watched by scouts from other clubs. A £1 million transfer took him to Anfield in July 1992 where he appeared nervous and unsure of the step up to the top division. He re-discovered his form and earned a call-up for the full England side, but further hesitant performances led to him joining Aston Villa and, away from the intense glare of publicity, finally began showing his early promise.

By the time he moved on to West Ham United he was established as the replacement for David Seaman and made the goalkeeper's berth his own for England and then moved to Manchester City after Seaman had announced his retirement following an injury. James seemed set for an extended run in the England side, but a couple of dodgy performances, culminating in a 2-2 draw against Austria in the first qualifying match for the 2006 World Cup in which he was at fault for at least one of the goals saw him relegated to the bench for England's next match away in Poland. Further poor performances during a tour of the United States in 2005 and a friendly against Denmark in August the same year saw him dropped from the squad altogether.

A move to Portsmouth in August 2006 has rekindled his career (he helped the club win the FA Cup in 2008) and has seen him re-established as England's first choice keeper under Fabio Capello.

▲ David James of Portsmouth saves at the feet of Anelka of Chelsea.

Juventus

▶ Happy Juventus players after scoring against Cagliari.

One of the greatest club sides in Italy, if not the whole of Europe, Juventus was formed in Turin by students from the D'Azeglio Lyceum in 1897. The club was initially known as Augusta Taurinorum but soon changed to the more recognisable Juventus.

According to legend, the club adopted pink shirts and black trousers (this being the days before shorts) as their club colours, and retained this rather bizarre outfit for the next six years. In 1903 they adopted black stripes.

A little more than a year later, Juventus won their first Italian league title. They were unable to build upon this success and the next 20 or so years were particularly barren, making the club ripe for a takeover. It was the Agnelli family, owners of the Fiat company in the city, that emerged triumphant, installing Eduardo Agnelli as president of the club in 1923. No expense was to be spared turning Juventus into the top club in Italy and there was an almost immediate return on their investment, Juve picking up their second title in 1925-26.

Eduardo was to remain president until his death in a plane accident in 1935, by which time Juve had registered seven league titles, including five on the trot between 1930-31 and 1934-35. Although Fiat money continued to pour into the club after the death of Eduardo Agnelli, his loss seemed to affect the club on the pitch and they were not to win another title until 1949-50.

They had by that time collected their first Italian Cup wins in 1938 and 1942, but Juventus' chief period of domination was to come in the 1970s and 80s, winning no fewer than nine league titles in 14 years. To date Juventus has won the Italian league title on 28 occasions – their nearest rivals are AC Milan with a mere 17. Add nine Cup and four Italian Super Cup wins and they are easily the most successful domestic side.

This success has been equalled by their exploits in Europe. Three times winners of the UEFA Cup, Juventus became the first side to have won all three major European trophies with victory in the Cup Winners' Cup in 1984 and the European Cup the following year. Of course, the European Cup victory has come to be remembered for all the wrong

reasons after events at the Heysel Stadium in the final, but there is no doubting that this was a special side complete with such illustrious names as Platini, Zoff and Rossi.

Juventus' last success in Europe was victory in the UEFA Champions League in 1996, achieved with a 4-2 penalty win over Ajax after extra time. Fabio Capello (the current England manager) became manager in 2004, and led Juventus to two more Serie A titles. But during May 2006, Juventus were one of five clubs linked to a Serie A match fixing scandal, the result of which saw the club relegated to Serie B for the first time in their history, as well as being stripped of the two titles won under Capello. Many key players were sold, however, other big name players remained to help the club return to Serie A. The season was notable because Alessandro Del Piero broke club records, by becoming the first Juventus player to appear 500 times in all competitions for the club. The bianconeri were promoted straight back up as league winners after the 2006-07 season. Since their return to Serie A in the 2007-08 season former Chelsea manager Claudio Ranieri has been at the helm. They finished in 3rd place in their first return season and qualified for the 2008-09 Champions League – back where they belong. Juventus is arguably the best supported football club in the world with over 11 million national fans (28 per cent of Italian football fans) and a further 170 million worldwide.

Keegan

▶ Keegan celebrates a goal for England against Brazil, 1978.

▶▶ Disgruntled Keegan fans demonstrate at Newcastle.

Whilst Kevin Keegan may not have been the most naturally gifted player to have represented England, he was certainly one of the hardest working. His rise at Liverpool after being signed by Bill Shankly in 1971 was little short of phenomenal. During his time at Anfield he won winner's medals in the FA Cup (1974), European Cup (1977), UEFA Cup (1973 and 1976) and three league titles (1973, 1976 and 1977) and was named Footballer of the Year in 1976. He surprisingly elected to leave Liverpool in June 1977, signing for SV Hamburg although the move had little effect on his standing within the game, for in 1978 and 1979 he was named European Player of the Year, also collecting the German Player of the Year award in 1978. He helped Hamburg win the Bundesliga Championship in 1979 and the following year was inspirational as they reached the European Cup final, although they were beaten by Liverpool, for whom Kenny Dalglish, his replacement at Anfield, was in excellent form.

He returned to England in July 1980, linking with Lawrie McMenemy at Southampton, and whilst domestic honours eluded the Saints, Keegan was again named Footballer of the Year in 1982. He left Southampton the same year in order to galvanise Newcastle United's promotion push, costing the club £100,000 but repaying the fee when promotion was secured in 1984.

In 1992, after eight years out of the game he came back into the limelight

by accepting the position of manager of his beloved Newcastle United. His impact at St James' Park matched what he had achieved as a player, guiding the club to the First Division Championship and promotion into the Premier League. They then became chief rivals to Manchester United for the league title although had to be content with a runners-up spot.

In January 1997 Keegan sensationally resigned and was, once again, replaced by Kenny Dalglish. After a brief spell as a television pundit Keegan returned to the game with Fulham, accepting an invitation to become director of football. He set them on the road to the Premier League, but by the time they arrived, he was already elsewhere. Following the departure of Glenn Hoddle from the England manager's position, he was seen as the ideal replacement and guided the team to the finals of the 2000 European Championships. Germany was to loom large again a few months later, for in England's opening game of the 2002 World Cup qualifying campaign, the Germans won 1-0 in the last game played at the old Wembley stadium. Keegan tendered his resignation immediately after the game, saying he had taken the team as far as he could.

After a short spell at Manchester City, in 2005, with his contract due to expire at the end of the season, he announced that he would not be renewing it as he wanted to retire.

He had been out of football for almost three years when he sensationally returned to Newcastle United for a second spell as manager in January 2008. This latest episode only lasted eight months, however, as Keegan resigned in September 2008 following a dispute with the club directors.

Keepers

▶ Gordon Banks of Leicester, Stoke and England.

▶▶ Bert Trautmann leaves the field after playing the 1956 FA Cup final with a broken neck.

England has produced some excellent goalkeepers down the years, the finest of whom was probably Gordon Banks. He played in 73 full internationals and, amongst his many memorable saves, was the one from Pelé in the 1970 World Cup. Neither Pelé, nor anybody else, could believe it when Banks tipped that particular shot over the bar.

Ray Clemence won 61 England caps, and would have played for his country more often had it not been for the emergence of Peter Shilton who won a total of 125 caps and also played in a remarkable 1,005 league games prior to his retirement in 1997.

Until the late 1980s it was quite unusual to see a foreign born goalkeeper or, for that matter, any other player, turning out for an English league side. Manchester City did however have an acrobatic and brave foreign keeper many years earlier. He was Bernhardt Trautmann, a former German prisoner of war, who guarded City's net between 1949 and 1964. Trautmann is famous for having broken his neck in the 1956 FA Cup final – and playing on. Today, at least half of the keepers playing regularly in the Premier League are of foreign origin. Chelsea's Petr Cech is arguably the best; he holds an English Premier League record of not conceding a goal in 1,025 minutes, and the most clean sheets in a single Premier League season (25), set during Chelsea's 2004-05 title-winning campaign. Not far behind is Manchester United's Edwin van der Sar, the most capped Dutch player of all time, who joined the club in 2005

and has since helped United secure their second successive Premier League title and win the Champions League by saving the final shootout penalty from Chelsea's Nicolas Anelka.

The position of England's Number One is somewhat up for grabs. Blackburn's Paul Robinson was seen as the long-term incumbent but a succession of high-profile errors reduced his confidence and that of the national team manager's to trust him between the sticks. Debutant Scott Carson was unfairly thrown into his first competitive international match by manager Steve McClaren against Croatia in a vital European Championships' qualifier at Wembley and it was his mistake when he let in a speculative long shot from Croatia's Niko Kranjcar that led to the team's surprise defeat and exit from the 2008 tournament. Portsmouth's David James was back for the start of the 2010 World Cup qualifiers but at nearly 40 years of age his tenure will not last long. West Ham's Robert Green seems to have been harshly overlooked while young keepers such as Ben Foster and Joe Hart are not yet ready. For a country that for decades boasted the best international goalkeepers in the world it is a transitional period until we find a new Banks or Shilton.

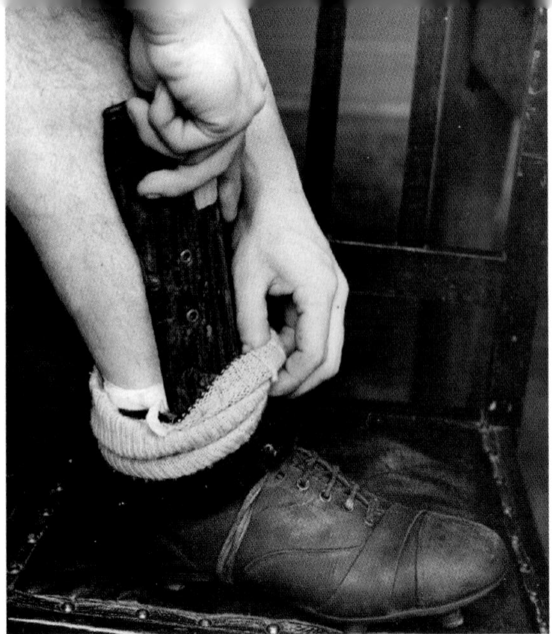

▲ The old fashioned football boot with nailed in studs.

▶ David Beckham's boots.

Kit

As Britain had been the home of football, most of the early kit manufacturers came from that territory. A glance at any early programme will reveal apparel that is totally alien to today's streamlined kits.

The first major kit manufacturer in the UK was Umbro, a company set up by brothers Wallace and Harold Humphreys in Wilmslow in Cheshire in 1924. Within 10 years Umbro had moved into supplying professional clubs, kitting out FA Cup winners Manchester City in 1934 and Sheffield Wednesday a year later. Umbro's influence extended beyond these shores and they were suppliers to the great Brazilian sides of 1958, 1962 and 1970. In 1966 Umbro supplied 15 of the 16 qualifiers for the World Cup finals in England, including hosts and winners England.

A year after Umbro first opened for business, German Adolf Dassler began making athletic shoes. He called his company Adidas, Adi being his family nickname and "das" the first three letters of his surname. He chose three stripes as his company logo because that was how many sons he had. Whilst Adidas is still the largest supplier of athletic shoes in the world, it is with football kit that their reputation has been made. Adi's brother Rudolf also moved into kit manufacture following a disagreement with his brother and launched the Puma company, another major player in the market.

The most important development in recent years has been the arrival of the American company Nike. Formed in 1971 by Phil Knight and Jeff Johnson, the company can trace its roots back a further 10 years when Knight and Bill Bowerman had been importers of Japanese sports equipment into the American market. Their success as importers prompted them to go into manufacturing, and within 10 years Nike was the predominant brand in the US. The distinctive "swoosh", the brainchild of Caroline Davidson, depicts the wing of the Greek goddess of victory Nike from which the company got their name.

Just before the opening of the 1994 World Cup finals in America, Nike signed a sponsorship deal with the Brazilian football federation which prompted a number of other countries to sign up with them.

Players and former players have become increasingly involved in the design of boots, with Craig Johnston, the former Liverpool and Australia player, being responsible for the Predator boot.

Manufactured by Adidas and worn by England centurion David Beckham, the Predator has become one of the most popular football boot's of the current age. With "blades" instead of studs and a hefty pricetag, it typifies both the refinement and rewards associated with today's kit.

Lineker

▶ Gary Lineker of England in action during the World Cup, 1990.

Gary Winston Lineker, Leicester's most famous crisp muncher, was born on 30th November 1960 – his second name reflecting the fact that he was born on Churchill's birthday. Whilst at school, young Gary was an accomplished all round sportsman and, in a report, one of his teachers wrote, "He must devote less time to sport if he wants to be a success." The teacher got it wrong.

Lineker joined Leicester City and went on to play 209 games and score 103 goals. He then transferred to Everton where, in the short time he was at Goodison, he made 57 appearances, scoring on 40 occasions but missed out on both the league and FA Cup honours to Liverpool, although he did win Footballer of the Year awards from both the writers' and players' associations.

He then went to Mexico with the England squad and won the "Golden Boot" for finishing the competition's top goalscorer, which alerted Europe's top clubs as to his talents. A £2.75 million deal took him to Barcelona where he won domestic and European honours, the latter in the European Cup Winners' Cup. He moved back to Britain in

1989, linking up with former Barcelona manager Terry Venables at Spurs and two years later won his first major honour in the domestic game, an FA Cup winner's medal (despite becoming only the second player to miss a penalty in an FA Cup final at Wembley).

He won his first England cap in 1984 and finished his England career with 80 caps and 48 goals, one goal agonisingly short of Bobby Charlton's record, which he might have equalled but for an uncharacteristic penalty miss against Brazil. At the end of the 1991–92 season he moved on from Spurs to Japan to help launch the Japanese league, although a niggling toe injury later forced him to retire from playing. He was a superb ambassador for the game (he was never booked) and his country, and was awarded the OBE in 1992. He is now a television presenter for the BBC hosting its flagship *Match of the Day* programme.

▲ Gary Lineker evades Scotland's Alex McLeish in 1988 during one of his 80 games for England.

Liverpool

Liverpool Football Club was founded on 15th March 1892. Anfield has been the club's only home, but Everton originally played there before moving to Goodison Park. Liverpool first won the League Championship in 1901, and they have won it 18 times in all.

The club's most famous manager was undoubtedly the remarkable Bill Shankly. He took over at Anfield in December 1959 and remained in charge for almost 15 years. Liverpool were in the old Second Division when Shankly, a former Scotland international wing-half, joined them from Huddersfield Town, but they went on to become a very good side indeed. Bill Shankly was sometimes criticised for not bringing on enough home-grown youngsters, but amongst his most important signings were two players from Scunthorpe United – Kevin Keegan and goalkeeper Ray Clemence. The foundations were laid for the most exciting time in Liverpool's history.

When Shankly resigned, he was replaced by his assistant, the equally remarkable Bob Paisley. During Paisley's nine-year tenure, Liverpool won the League Championship six times, the European Cup three times, and the UEFA Cup once. They also won the League Cup three times although the FA Cup eluded them. The club had continued success under Joe Fagan and

Kenny Dalglish, but their supremacy did not last for ever.

Two tragedies had a serious effect on the club and on its supporters. In May 1985, 39 Italian fans died when a wall collapsed at the Heysel Stadium in Belgium, whilst Liverpool were playing Juventus in the European Cup final. This led to Liverpool being banned from European competition for a decade but then, just four years later, 97 Liverpool supporters were killed in the Hillsborough disaster during an FA Cup semi-final against Nottingham Forest – a tragedy which changed the face of English football.

A succession of relatively unsuccessful managers in the 1990s – Graeme Souness, Roy Evans and Gerard Houllier – were forgotten when, in May 2005, Spaniard Rafael Benitez capped his first season in charge with a stunning European Cup win, the Reds overturning a three-goal deficit against AC Milan to triumph on penalties thanks to inspirational skipper Steven Gerrard. Incredibly, he did it again with Benitez guiding the team to the Champions League final in 2007, where they lost 2–1 to AC Milan.

The fans though are becoming restless for a Premier League title but even with such world-class players as Spain's Fernando Torres and Gerrard the team lack consistency and under Benitez have looked unable to compete against Manchester United and Chelsea until recently.

◀ Rafael Benitez giving a press conference at Anfield.

◀◀ Alan Kennedy holding the European Cup.

Maradona

▶ Argentina's Diego Maradona as he should be remembered in his playing prime.

▶▶ Maradona brandishes the World Cup won by his team after a 3-2 victory over West Germany, 1986.

Striker Diego Armando Maradona's career took him from Buenos Aires' slums to the captaincy of his country, leading Argentina to 3-2 victory over Germany in the World Cup final of 1986. Sadly, like the similarly gifted George Best and Paul Gascoigne, the tale was to end in tragedy.

Having made his professional debut age 15 and taken his international bow a mere six months later, Maradona left Boca Juniors for Spanish giants Barcelona in 1982. There his ankle was badly broken and, it's believed, he sought solace in drugs for the first time. He joined Napoli in 1984 for a then world record £4.1 million, transforming a mediocre team and leading them to two Championships and the UEFA Cup amid much hero-worship from their hard-core "tifosi" fans. Together with the Mexico World Cup, where he scored the infamous "Hand of God" goal against England en route to final victory, this was undoubtedly the period when Maradona played his finest football.

His fortunes in four World Cups

graphically illustrated his rise and fall. In 1982, he had been sent off in Spain for youthful frustration (though his £1.7 million transfer to Barcelona followed), while eight years later in Italy he again managed to steer his country to the final. But an early exit from the 1994 tournament followed a positive drugs test and his team flopped in the absence of their talismanic captain.

Leaving Italy in 1991, the year he failed his first drugs test, Maradona returned home via Seville and retired in 1997 on his 37th birthday shortly after a third drugs bust. Three years later he went to Cuba in an attempt to recover his health.

In 2004 he was admitted to a private clinic in Buenos Aires in a critical condition, suffering high blood pressure and respiratory failure. Since then he has struggled with self-induced health problems and the world watches with baited breath hoping that he doesn't go the way of a Gascoigne or a Best.

Many still consider Maradona a better player than Pelé – acknowledged by FIFA as the best ever player – and, despite his problems, he is held in great affection by football followers with a 20,000-strong worldwide fan club.

Matthews

▼ Stanley Matthews outside-right for England and Blackpool FC.

Stanley Matthews was born in Hanley, one of Stoke's five towns, on 1st February 1915. He was the son of a professional boxer and he joined Stoke City as an outside-right in 1932. From the beginning, Matthews was an outstanding player. His body swerve and ball control became famous, and he was eventually to become known as the Wizard of the Dribble. Full-backs didn't stand a chance as Stanley ghosted past them and then proceeded to cross the ball with pin-point accuracy.

Matthews had been a schoolboy international, and he went on to play 54 times for England at senior level. He would have won many more caps today, but there were fewer international matches played in those days, and in any case the war intervened. In 1947, having played in 259 league games for Stoke, he moved to Blackpool for what now seems a paltry fee of £11,500. He had scored 51 league goals for his hometown club, but he had made many more. Matthews was to remain at Blackpool until 1961 when, at the age of 46, he went back to Stoke to see out his playing days, and help regain top division status.

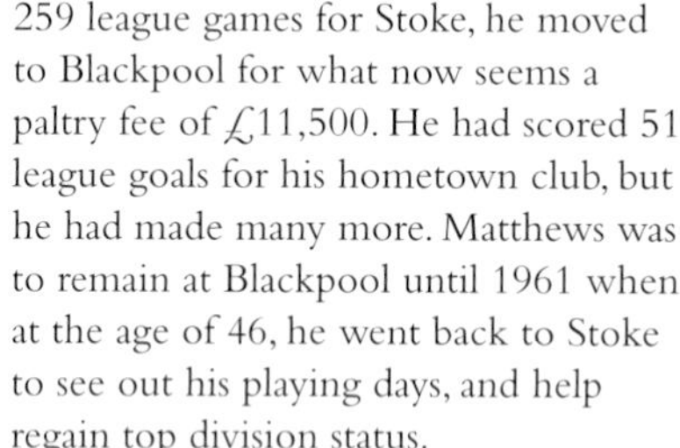

The highlight of Stanley Matthews' outstanding career had undoubtedly been what became known as the Matthews final. In 1953, Blackpool faced Bolton Wanderers at Wembley. It was probably Matthews' last chance of an FA Cup winner's medal, but at one stage his team was 3-1 down. Blackpool recovered to win 4-3, with Stanley Matthews creating two of their goals and Stan Mortensen scoring a hat-trick. Stanley M probably thought the game should have been called the Mortensen final, but you can bet he didn't care.

Stanley Matthews, a modest man who liked a pint or three, continued playing past his 50th birthday. He never earned more than about £75 a week and he made his last appearance for Stoke City in 1965. In that same year, he became Sir Stanley. He died aged 85, in the year 2000.

Moore

Bobby Moore was probably the most influential captain ever to have served club and country and his death from cancer was mourned nationwide, irrespective of club allegiances. After starring as a schoolboy, Bobby signed for his local West Ham club as a professional in June 1958 and represented England at Youth level the following season.

His assured and polished performances soon made him a regular at half-back in the West Ham side and he quickly became captain. In a three-year spell during the 1960s he collected three of the game's greatest prizes, all at Wembley. In 1964 he inspired West Ham to overcome plucky Preston in the FA Cup final (the same year as he was named Footballer of the Year), 12 months later to the European Cup Winners' Cup against TSV Munich and then, in 1966, was captain as England won the World Cup.

His performances during the 1966 tournament were exceptional; four years later he had become perhaps the best defensive half-back in the world, as the 1970 tournament was to prove.

▲ Bobby Moore of England poses for a photograph during a training session, 1965.

The campaign hardly began with an auspicious start, for he was arrested in Colombia and falsely accused of stealing a gold bracelet from a jewellers in the city of Bogota, but after a spell under house-arrest at the British Embassy rejoined his team-mates in Mexico preparing for the World Cup. Moore quickly demonstrated that the fuss had not unsettled him, and his performance against future world champions Brazil was perhaps the most accomplished ever seen on the world stage, a fact acknowledged by Pelé who made immediate tracks for Moore at the final

▲ Bobby Moore pictured as captain of West Ham, first of his two London clubs.

whistle to warmly shake his hand.

Alf Ramsey kept faith with Moore until 1973, handing him a then record haul of 108 caps for England, and in 1973 Bobby moved across London to join Fulham after 544 league appearances for West Ham. Two years later Moore inspired Fulham to their first ever FA Cup final, ironically against West Ham at Wembley. There the fairytale ended, with West Ham winning 2-0.

Bobby was widely expected to move into management at the end of his playing career, but apart from brief spells with non-League Oxford City and later Southend United did not get a chance to realise his potential. It is pure speculation, of course, but the success enjoyed by the likes of West Germany who appointed Franz Beckenbauer with little or no managerial experience but still emerged as world champions inevitably lead to the conclusion that England should perhaps have taken a chance, especially after the barren years following Alf Ramsey's departure. As it was Bobby Moore was lost to the game he had graced for so long other than as a journalist, a role he held right up to his death.

Memories and stories of Bobby Moore are legendary; from the way he thoughtfully wiped his hand on his shirt before collecting the World Cup from Queen Elizabeth II, his speed of thought to blow the referee's whistle after the official had been knocked unconscious during a match at Upton Park in 1970, the time he was forced to go in goal during a League Cup semi-final and saved a penalty but, more than anything, the calm, authoritative way he went about playing his game. In addition to the 108 caps Bobby won playing for England, he also made one appearance *against* them, turning out for Team America in an unofficial friendly in Philadelphia in 1976.

Newcastle

Newcastle United was formed in 1892, following the merger of several local clubs. Throughout its proud history, the club has won the League Championship four times, and the FA Cup on six occasions. In recent times however, the record has not been quite so impressive. Newcastle last won the League Championship in 1927. During part of the 1980s, and again during the early 1990s, they were out of the top division and, although they were Premier League runners-up in 1996 and 1997 and FA Cup runners-up in 1974, 1998 and 1999, their last major honour was the Inter Cities Fairs Cup in 1969.

Kevin Keegan returned them to the top flight in 1993, but Kenny Dalglish found him a hard act to follow when he took over four years later. A succession of managers has followed including Bobby Robson, Graeme Souness, Glenn Roeder and Sam Allardyce.

King Kevin returned to St James' Park 11 years after he had left, being appointed by Mike Ashley who became hated by the fans. He was even more loathed when Keegan walked out.

Supporters would love their former star striker Alan Shearer to take over the reins as manager but while the club is in such turmoil he still waits in the wings for the right time to return.

▲ Skipper Bobby Moncur displays Newcastle's last major trophy, the Inter Cities Fairs Cup, won in 1969.

▲ Kingsley, the very unroyal looking Reading mascot.

Nicknames

Who do you support? The Spireites, Cobblers, Rams or Bantams? Fans of Chesterfield, Northampton, Derby County and Bradford City know who we're talking about – we are, of course, talking nicknames.

Most tend to stick – hence Fulham will always be the Cottagers wherever they end up playing on a permanent basis. Similarly Sheffield Wednesday's "Owls" appellation results from their Hillsborough ground being known as Owlerton until 1912. Bristol Rovers' Eastville home, which they left in 1986, was next to a gasworks, a fact mocked by Bristol City fans but taken up as a badge of pride by Rovers' Gasheads. (The official nickname of the club was and remains the Pirates.)

Some labels like Liverpool's "Reds" or Tottenham Hotspurs' "Spurs" are mundane. More original nicknames resulting from the club colours include the Canaries of Norwich with their bright yellow shirts and Queens Park Rangers, traditionally the Rs, who have recently become the Super Hoops due to their blue and white hooped jerseys. There's a striped Everton Mint, and the club are known as the Toffees, but their shirts remain deepest blue.

Tradition plays a major part. West Bromwich Albion was formed as a works team for the local iron works where the foundry workers' trousers were known as Baggies. But the origins can get lost with the passage of time. Charlton's Addicks appellation comes either from the haddock which the team loved eating or the fact that, with commendable hospitality, they took their opponents for a fish supper after games. Take your pick – or you can just call them the Valiants!

Nicknames can change; Reading were known as the Biscuitmen but, after biscuit-making in the area declined in the 1970s, Royals was chosen as its replacement – perhaps because Berkshire is where Windsor Castle is situated.

Once the Rokerites, Sunderland became the Black Cats after a competition that coincided with their departure from Roker Park in 1997. Newcastle fans call them the Mackems, a term of abuse deriving from the days when Sunderland was a leading shipbuilding town. During the day, it's said, the shipbuilders built the ships, and during the night they would indulge in a little light-fingered "piracy".

Using the dialect of the time, people – no doubt from Newcastle – said of the Sunderland men, "They maak 'em then taak 'em" (make them then take them). Somehow, the first part has stuck! Similarly Portsmouth fans call their Southampton neighbours Scummers after Southampton dock workers apparently broke a strike.

Perhaps the nicest nickname source is Bury's Shakers. When asked about his team's chances against mighty Blackburn Rovers in the 1892 Lancashire Cup final, club chairman J T Ingham was reported to have said, "We'll shake 'em!"

They did, 2-0!

▼ Sheffields Wednesday's Owl mascot reflects their location derived nickname.

▲ Doncaster Rovers on the up, here beating Leeds United to secure promotion to the Championship, May 2008.

Non-League

Non-League football in England is played at a level below that of the Premier League and the Football League. Typically it has been played on an amateur or semi-professional basis, but in recent years full professionalism has become the norm in the Football Conference, the next rung of the ladder down from the 92 Premier and Football League clubs.

The term non-League was commonly used well before 1992 (when the Premier League was formed) when the top football clubs in England all belonged to the Football League; all clubs who were not a part of the Football League were classified as non-League clubs.

In Scotland, football outside the top four divisions consists of the Junior Leagues together with a number of Senior Leagues, although the term non-League is also commonly used – as it is throughout Europe.

The "League" of "non-League football" refers to the Football League, rather than leagues in general – indeed "non-League" clubs play most of their football in league competitions. There are numerous leagues below the level of the Football League, and some, such as the Northern league, are almost as old as the league itself. The most senior of these leagues are loosely organised by the Football Association, the sport's governing body in England, into a National League System (NLS). The NLS has seven levels or steps, and includes over 50 separate leagues, many with more than one division.

Prior to 1987 there was no automatic promotion and relegation between the Football League and the leagues of non-League football. The bottom clubs of the Football League were required to apply for re-election to the league at the end of the season, but this was in most cases a mere formality. The system ensured that Football League membership remained relatively static, with non-League clubs having almost no chance of joining. However major change came in 1987 when automatic promotion and relegation of one club between the Football League and the Football Conference, the top league in non-League football, was introduced, subject to the eligible club meeting the required facility and financial standards. Scarborough became the first non-League club to win automatic promotion to the Football League, and Lincoln City became the first league club to be relegated to the ranks of non-League football. Since 2003 two clubs from the Conference (the champions and the winners of a play-off) have been promoted at the end of each season.

There have been notable successes among the clubs which have graduated from non-League. Wimbledon, admitted in 1977 in place of Workington after 88 years of existence, were playing in the top flight within a decade (Workington, the team they replaced, never made it back), while Doncaster Rovers, who ascended in 2003, obtained successive promotions, underlining the parity between Third Division and Conference. Rushden and Diamonds, formed from the amalgamation of two Northamptonshire clubs, made it to the league in 2001 funded by footwear magnate Max Griggs' millions.

The entire English football league system includes the Premier League, the Football League, the NLS leagues, and any local leagues that have feeder relationships with an NLS league. In women's football, the non-League term is used for those clubs in the divisions below the FA Women's Premier League's two regional second divisions.

▼ Rushden and Diamonds players acclaim their fans after ascending to the league, 2001.

Oldest Players

▶ Sir Stanley Matthews who carried on playing to the age of 50.

The game's oldest players are a lot older than they used to be! Modern fitness regimes and diets are allowing players to stay fitter longer and continue at the top level. It helps if you didn't have much pace to begin with – for example Gary Speed, David Beckham, Paul Scholes – as their minds are thinking just as fast as ever as they hold back the sands of time.

Goalkeepers, of course, have a natural advantage as they are not required to run around much in the first place and the greatest examples of longevity in the game are usually guardians of the sticks. Indeed, the record for England's greatest number of caps (125) is held by goalkeeper Peter Shilton who also played more than 1000 league games in a career spanning 30 years while David James, the current England keeper, has played more than 650 games over a 20 year career which is still going strong at Portsmouth.

The oldest-ever English footballer was Sir Stanley Matthews who played his final game for Stoke City on 6th February 1965 aged 50 years and 4 days old. The oldest player in Premier League history was madcap goalkeeper John Burridge. He was playing for Manchester City aged 43 years, 4 months and 26 days old when he played against Newcastle United on April 29th, 1995. Teddy Sheringham can lay claim to have been the oldest outfield who played in the Premier League, at 40 years and 270 days. This record may be broken by Dean Windass who is still playing for Hull City and will be 40 on April 1st 2009.

If you're ever asked who was the oldest player of all time in a pub quiz, chances are the answer will be Roy of the Rovers who played for the same club for more than 40 years scoring 5000 goals!

Ooh Aah Cantona

▲ Eric Cantona, 1994.

During his long and successful career in management, Alex Ferguson has bought many exciting players. Of all the deals the Scot has done, none have turned out to be as important as the one he did in taking Eric Cantona across the M62 for £1 million in 1992.

Born in Marseille on 24th May 1966, Eric joined Auxerre in 1981 and made his debut in 1983. After completing his national service Eric was loaned out to Second Division club Martigues to gain first team experience. He returned to Auxerre and signed professional forms in 1986, soon after representing his country at Under-21 and full level. In June 1988 he was transferred to Olympique Marseille for £2.3 million, but the move soon turned sour, not least because Eric has never been afraid to speak his mind.

Unable to gain his place in the side once he had recovered from injury, he was sold to Nimes-Olympique for £1 million and was soon back into trouble with the authorities. Hauled before a disciplinary committee for throwing a ball at a referee, Cantona was given a one-month ban. When he then went up to each committee member in turn and told them they were all idiots, this was doubled! Eric Cantona announced his immediate retirement from the game in December 1991.

He was persuaded to give it one last go in England and came over to talk to Sheffield Wednesday. Wednesday were unwilling to sign him without a trial so he headed up the M1 to talk to Leeds United. Howard Wilkinson signed the player on the spot and Eric repaid him by helping Leeds United win the league title at the end of the 1991-92 season.

▲ Eric Cantona (centre right) celebrates with his team-mates after scoring his first goal against Chelsea during the FA Cup final, 1994.

The fans took him to their hearts, coming up with the "Ooh aah Cantona" chant and turning him into a cult hero.

His surprise departure across the Pennines to sign for Manchester United saw him become the first player to win consecutive league titles with different clubs. The following year United retained their title and won the FA Cup to boot, only the fourth Double of the modern era.

They should have repeated the feat again in 1995, but Cantona was an enforced absentee. Once again, it was his temperament that had caused the problem; reacting to taunting from a section of the crowd during United's clash with Crystal Palace, he had leapt the barrier and kung fu kicked the fan with the biggest mouth! A seven-month ban and £10,000 fine were handed out by the football authorities, whilst the legal system subsequently handed him a two-week jail term, later reduced to 120 hours' community service.

With Cantona back in the side in November 1995, Manchester United returned to winning ways, landing another Double at the end of the season. That Eric should have been the man responsible for scoring the only goal of the FA Cup final against Liverpool was the icing on the cake. At the end of the season he was named Football Writers' Player of the Year.

Eric collected his fourth and final league title medal with United at the end of the 1996-97 season, meaning he had won league titles in five out of the previous six years. Not a bad return for a player who had initially announced his retirement in 1991. Eric announced it again at the end of the season, and now spends his time acting or singing or managing beach soccer teams!

Owen

One of the brightest talents to have emerged in the English game in many a year, Michael Owen signed with Liverpool as a junior, despite being an Everton fan as a youngster. He made an immediate impact at Liverpool, scoring on his debut when called off the bench away at Wimbledon and quickly established himself in the side following Robbie Fowler's long term injury.

His phenomenal pace and eye for goal demanded a call-up for the full England side and on 11th February 1998 he was selected for the match against Chile, becoming England's youngest international player this century; at 18 years and 59 days he beat Duncan Edwards' record by 124 days.

He was part of the squad for the 1998 World Cup finals, scoring against Romania after coming on as a substitute and netting a breathtaking goal in the clash with Argentina in the second round. He quickly added further goals and seemed on course to seriously challenge the likes of Gary Lineker and Bobby Charlton as England's top goalscorer, netting 30 goals for his country in just 60 appearances.

In the summer of 2004 however he refused to sign an extension to his Liverpool contract, citing his unhappiness at the Reds not mounting a serious title challenge. Rather than let him eventually leave on a free transfer Liverpool sold him to Spanish giants Real Madrid for a cut-price £8 million. He spent much of his first season at the Bernabeu Stadium sitting on the bench but was invariably introduced at some stage during games and made his point by netting 18 goals for the club in just over 40 appearances.

The arrival of additional strikers to the club spelt the end of Owen's time with Real Madrid, and although overtures were made to Liverpool about signing him back, he eventually moved to Newcastle United for £17 million on transfer deadline day, 31st August 2005. Injuries have restricted his club and international appearances since then although he remains England's fourth highest scorer of all time.

▲ Michael Owen in action for Newcastle against Everton.

Owners

▲ Manchester City's previous owner Thaksin Shinawatra sits next to team manager Sven Goran Eriksson.

When football was in its infancy, all manner of businessmen got attracted into funding a club. Invariably there were sound business reasons for so doing; John Houlding had invested in Everton in order to provide thirsty customers for his premises near their ground at Anfield, Sandon Hotel. Similarly, Spurs' move into White Hart Lane was assisted by the brewers Charrington who had noticed great takings at public houses near football grounds.

As football grew, the directors saw their role in a different light. Now, being a member of the board at a successful club was seen as something of a status symbol.

Perhaps the most famous football dynasty in England had been the Edwards family at Manchester United, with butcher Louis Edwards passing on control of the club to his son Martin (who subsequently sold out). Similarly, the Agnelli family in Turin had bought into Juventus in the 1920s, a connection they retain to this day. A successful Juventus side, and they've had plenty of those over the years, ensures a happy workforce at the Fiat plant come Monday and increased production.

Buying into a football club doesn't always have to break the bank. Ken Bates bought control of Chelsea, after previously being involved with Oldham Athletic, for just £1, but he did have to guarantee their considerable debts into the bargain! While Bates developed Stamford Bridge into Chelsea Village, others have built new grounds, for example John Madejski (Reading), Dave Whelan (Wigan's JJB Stadium) and Firoz Kassam (Oxford).

It was Spurs who first came up with the idea of floating a club on the Stock Exchange as a means of raising revenue.

Their reasoning at the time, back in 1983, was that just about every other industry, including a fair few from the entertainment sector, was listed on the Stock Exchange, so why not football clubs? At first the scheme was a success; the flotation was over-subscribed, a number of institutional investors had picked up shares and there were dividends paid for each of the next seven or so years.

But football is not like most other businesses. A club's fortunes off the field are almost directly linked to its fortunes on it. A bad run of results will drive some of the floating supporters away, revenues will drop and profits will fall. Whilst the fan will not contemplate selling his meagre shareholding, retaining it for sentimental reasons and to feel he owns a bit of the club, the institutional investors are in it purely for the return.

It seems now that super-rich overseas investors are queuing up to purchase a trophy Premier League club – for example, the Abu Dhabi Investment Group's purchase of Manchester City in September 2008 – as much for the cudos than the love of the game.

As the *Daily Telegraph*'s Patrick Barclay commented, "What are they up to, these men? Sooner or later, we shall discover and the only sure thing, given the Government's continued turning of a blind eye to the most important issues in the most important sport, is that it will be too late, probably after the Premier League has reached the stage when enough of its owners are men with no real love of their clubs, or indeed English football in many instances, to outvote the others and relocate the league to, for example, Dubai, where it could form the basis of a World Football League."

▼ Former Chelsea owner Ken Bates with manager Claudio Ranieri. Both men, sadly, fell from favour on Abramovich's arrival.

Pelé

▶ Brazilian footballer Pelé in training for Brazil's match against England.

▶▶ Pelé scores the equalising goal for the Allied POW's during the match against Germany in Paris featured in the filming of *Escape to Victory*.

Widely regarded as the finest player in the world, Edson Arantes do Nascimento, or Pelé as he is better known, was born in Tres Coracoes, Brazil on 23rd October 1940. The son of a professional footballer, Pelé was spotted at the age of 13 as a potential star for the future and guided through Santos' youth team to senior status, making his debut at the age of 16. He was not yet 17 when he made his debut for Brazil. A knee injury shortly before the World Cup squad left for Sweden in 1958 threatened to keep him home, but he recovered sufficiently to play in four of Brazil's six games. He scored six goals in the tournament, including two in the final itself against Sweden.

The next two tournaments were personal disasters for Pelé; injured in the second game in 1962 he took no further part, although Brazil retained their trophy, and in 1966 brutal tackling by the Bulgarians and Portuguese saw both Pelé and Brazil off. He reached his peak in 1970 in Mexico, displaying alertness and skill levels never previously seen and scored four times during the competition.

After retiring from the international scene in 1971 he spent three further years with Santos before heading to the United States and New York Cosmos, single-handedly popularising the game in the US. He retired for good in 1977, having played 1,363 matches scoring 1,281 goals, including 97 for Brazil. At a time when all of his compatriots were heading to Europe to make their

fortunes, Pelé remained faithful to Santos, a decision that reinforced his reputation at home. On the world stage, he is equally revered, as evidenced by his honorary knighthood from Queen Elizabeth II in 1997 and the fact that he was coaxed out of retirement one final time in the early 1980s to play a starring role in the Michael Caine and Sylvester Stallone film *Escape To Victory*. Similar cameo appearances have seen him in *Mike Bassett: England Manager* and he was the face and voice of a worldwide Viagra campaign!

▶ A missed penalty from Beckham and England lost in the European Nations Championship 2004.

Penalties

As hard as it is to imagine now, the early law-makers of the game did not include the provision of a penalty into their rules simply because they did not believe that anyone playing the game would try to do anything untoward to obtain an advantage, especially around the goal area. The launch of the FA Cup in 1872 and the Football League in 1888 soon changed all that!

It was perhaps the experiences of Stoke that led to the two most vital changes in the games' laws. In 1890, during an FA Cup quarter-final with Notts County, a goal-bound Stoke shot was punched away by a County defender with the result that Stoke were awarded a free kick on the County goal-line. The resulting kick was easily blocked and County went on to win the match.

Although the Irish FA had introduced the penalty kick in 1890, the English and Scottish FAs did not follow suit until the following year, no doubt influenced by reports from the Notts County and Stoke match. Stoke were to suffer again during that first season, they were 2-1 down to Aston Villa late in the game when they were awarded a penalty

and the chance to equalise.

A Villa player grabbed hold of the ball and booted it out of the stadium; by the time it was retrieved the referee had blown for full time! Not surprisingly, the laws were amended to allow time for a penalty to be taken.

History records that Alex McCall of Renton scored the very first penalty, against Leith Athletic in August 1891. Three weeks later John Heath of Wolverhampton Wanderers became the first player to score a penalty in an English game, netting in the 5-0 win over Accrington on 14th September.

It was Pelé who announced that a penalty was a cowardly way to score a goal (although it did not stop him netting the 1,000th goal of his professional career from the penalty spot!) and there were those who held similar views; well-known amateur club Corinthian Casuals, according to legend, have never scored from the penalty spot in their long and distinguished history, deliberately missing every one since they believe in gentlemanly conduct.

In the hundred years or so that have followed, the course of football history has been changed on the award of a penalty and the subsequent outcome of the resulting kick. Huddersfield Town became the first club to win the FA Cup thanks to a heatedly debated penalty award against Preston North End in 1927.

The same club had benefited three years earlier when a Cardiff City penalty against Birmingham City was saved, allowing Huddersfield to collect the League Championship, whilst both John Aldridge (for Liverpool against Wimbledon in 1989) and Gary Lineker (for Spurs against Nottingham Forest in 1991) saw their penalties saved in FA Cup finals at Wembley. Lineker suffered again the following year, for his penalty in a friendly international against Brazil was similarly saved denying him a share of the record for England's leading goalscorer with Sir Bobby Charlton.

It was the Watney Cup, a pre-season tournament of the early 1970s, that first experimented with the idea of a penalty shootout, whereby each side would take five penalties apiece at the end of a drawn game in order to decide the result. Since then the destiny of all of the major tournaments has been decided by the penalty shootout with England probably holding the record as the worst practitioners of the art!

▲ Players from all around the world in the Chelsea team.

Premier League

The influx of television money into the game by the end of the 1980s had led many of the leading (for which you should read First Division) clubs to believe that they should receive a bigger share. Up until then the money was fairly evenly divided, with even the Fourth Division clubs, whose matches were seldom, if ever, shown live on television receiving a considerable sum.

By the turn of the decade, the leading clubs had had enough and 15 met at the FA's headquarters at Lancaster Gate in June 1991 to discuss the setting up of a Premier League under the control of the FA rather than the Football League. All agreed to resign from the Football League at the end of the season, with the rest of the First Division soon following suit. In January 1992 the FA council gave its seal of approval to a 22-team Premier League to commence season 1992-93, reducing to a 20-club division at the end of the 1994-95 season.

The new Premier League was able to offer, to the highest bidder, a flexible fixture schedule. One that would allow live matches to be played on a Sunday afternoon and Monday evening to begin with and, later on, matches played at 12 noon and 5.30pm on a Saturday.

With the Premier League awash with money, Chelsea's Roman Abramovich leading the way, there has been no shortage of world-class players eager to come and ply their trade in England, all well remunerated for their efforts. Thus the best that Brazil, Croatia, Slovenia, Moldova and Bulgaria has to offer can be found alongside somewhat less exotic heroes from England's traditional hunting grounds of Ireland, Scotland and Wales

Promoted as "The Greatest Show On Earth", the Premier League is the world's most popular and most watched sporting league, followed worldwide by over half a billion people in 202 countries, generally on networks owned and/or controlled by Sky or Setanta Sports.

Queen's Park

Founded on the south side of Glasgow in 1867, Queen's Park was, for many years, Scotland's premier football club. Its directors were instrumental in the formation of the Scottish Football Association.

As late as 1903, when Queen's Park played the inaugural match at their Hampden Park Stadium, the team was still a major force in Scottish football. That game, played before 44,530 spectators, resulted in a 1-0 win over local rivals Celtic. However, Queen's Park was a strictly amateur club and, by the turn of the century, professionalism had well and truly taken hold both north and south of the border. In one sense, the halcyon days were over, yet the club carried on into the 20th century and is still playing Scottish league football more than a hundred years later.

Perhaps the most remarkable thing of all is that Queen's Park continue to play at Hampden. Before the stadium was rebuilt during the 1990s, the club would play its league games with just a few hundred supporters standing on terraces which could accommodate upwards of 150,000 people. Hampden Park may be Scotland's national stadium, but the Scottish Football Association still has to lease it from a Third Division club – and an amateur one at that.

▲ A contemporary depiction of Queen's Park's defeat in the 1884 English FA Cup final against Blackburn Rovers.

Queens Park Rangers

▶ QPR celebrate after beating Charlton at The Valley.

Queens Park Rangers FC came into being around 1886, when a team called St Jude's was amalgamated with a team called Christchurch Rangers. The club has had a number of homes including, for two short spells, London's White City Stadium, but its supporters have always preferred Loftus Road.

QPR remained a Third Division (South) club until, in 1948, they topped the division and won promotion to the Second. Four years later they were relegated again, and they were to remain in Division Three until 1967.

The 1966-67 season was to prove a remarkable one for QPR. Not only did the team win the Third Division title, finishing 12 points clear of Middlesbrough, but they also won the first League Cup final to be played at Wembley. On that memorable day they were 2-0 down at one stage, but they went on to beat West Bromwich Albion 3-2. Just over a year later they were playing in the (old) First Division, but Rangers were relegated after just one season in the top flight.

Since those heady days, the fortunes of Queens Park Rangers have ebbed and flowed. They were founder members of the Premier League in 1992, but financial problems and various other difficulties at Loftus Road have seen them slide slowly down the league. QPR was bought by Formula One tycoons and multi-millionaires Bernie Ecclestone and Flavio Briatore in a £14 million takeover in August 2007. Four months later, billionaire Lakshmi Mittal purchased a 20 per cent shareholding in the club from Briatore.

Quickest Goals

◀ Hakan Sukur edges ahead of opponent Hong Myungbo en route to the World Cup's fastest ever goal, 2002.

As a goal can't be scored direct from the kick-off, the feat of British non-League footballer Marc Burrows who, in April 2004, scored the world's fastest-ever goal in just two seconds, is unlikely ever to be beaten.

Most "official" record books do not recognise this strike and credit Colin Cowperthwaite with Britain's fastest goal which was timed out in 3.55 seconds in 1979 for Barrow against Kettering in the Conference. The honour of scoring the fastest Premier League goal is shared by Ledley King (Tottenham) and Alan Shearer (Newcastle) at just 10 seconds. The fastest FA Cup final goal came from the boot of Roberto Di Matteo, who struck after just 43 seconds of Chelsea's 1997 Wembley win over Middlesbrough.

Gilberto Silva's lightning strike for Arsenal in Eindhoven came so quickly that even the official timekeepers initially missed it. At first, the Brazilian World Cup winner's well-taken strike was timed at 20.07 seconds, making it the second fastest goal in Champions League history.

The fastest goal in World Cup history was scored by Hakan Sukur in just 11 seconds in June. The Dutch claim the fastest World Cup final goal, Johan Neeskens' 80-second spot-kick scant consolation in the 1974 defeat by West Germany.

- *Quickest goal: 3.55 secs Colin Cowperthwaite (Barrow v Kettering 1979)*
- *Football League: 4 secs Jim Fryatt (Bradford PA v Tranmere 1964)*
- *Premier League: 10 secs Ledley King (Bradford v Spurs 2000)*
- *FA Cup final: 43 secs Roberto Di Matteo (Chelsea v Middlesbro' 1997)*
- *Champions League: 20.07 secs Gilberto Silva (PSV Eindhoven v Arsenal, 2002)*
- *World Cup: 11secs Hakan Sukur (Turkey v Korea 2002)*
- *World Cup final: 80 secs Johan Neeskens (Holland v Germany 1974)*

Real Madrid

A survey of newspaper editors around the world asked who was the biggest football club in the world. The majority answered Real Madrid despite the claims of Juventus and Manchester United.

Formed as Madrid FC in the late 1890s by students, the club has its official birth given as March 1902. In 1920 the club was granted the prefix Real, meaning Royal, by King Alfonso XIII and became founder members of the Spanish league in 1927 and have never been relegated out of the First Division.

Real Madrid's elevation to worldwide recognition can be traced back to 1943 with the appointment of Santiago Bernabeu as club president. A former player, coach and secretary of the club, Bernabeu's vision and fundraising abilities transformed the club on and off the pitch. He turned their ground at Chamartin from a crumbling relic that accommodated 14,000 in 1943 to a superb new stadium with room for 75,000 by 1949. During the 1950s, financed by European success, the Estadio Bernabeu could hold 125,000. Fans from across the country flocked to see some of the best players in the world – Hungarian Ferenc Puskas, Argentinean Alfredo Di Stefano and homegrown stars such as Francisco Gento.

Whilst they are undoubtedly the most successful side at home, having won the league title 31 times (their nearest rivals Barcelona can only muster 18) and the cup 17 times (here Barcelona and Athletic Bilbao hold sway, having won 24 and 23 times respectively), it is their unrivalled European success that has made their name. Winners of the European Cup in each of its first five seasons, they found further success in 1966, 1998, 2000 and 2002. Added to this are victories in the UEFA Cup in 1985 and 1986, in the process becoming the first side to retain the trophy. The only European trophy to elude them was the European Cup Winners' Cup, but only just, for they were beaten finalists in 1971 and 1983.

In July 2000, Florentino Pérez was

▲ Bernd Schuster gives instructions to his team before a training session.

elected club president with a promise to sign Luis Figo. The following year, the club controversially sold its training ground and used the money to begin assembling the famous Galáctico side including players such as Zidane, Ronaldo, Roberto Carlos, Raúl González and David Beckham. It is debatable whether the gamble paid off, as despite a European Cup win in 2002, followed by the league in 2003, the club failed to win a major trophy for the next three seasons.

Ramón Calderón was elected as club president in July 2006 and subsequently appointed Fabio Capello as the new coach. Real Madrid won the La Liga title in 2007 for the first time in four years but despite this achievement Capello was dismissed (and went off to manage England) being replaced by German manager and former player Bernd Schuster.

The Whites ended the 2007-08 season with the 31st league title and the first consecutive league title in 18 years. They also established a new La Liga record by scoring 85 points. If they can capture the Champions League, normal service will have been resumed.

▲ Cristiano Ronaldo is congratulated by team-mates after scoring his team's fifth goal and completing his first hat-trick.

Ronaldo

Cristiano Ronaldo is one of Manchester United's greatest ever players. He became United's first ever Portuguese player when he signed for £12.24 million after the 2002-03 season. He asked for the squad number 28 (his number at Sporting) as he did not want the pressure of living up to the expectation linked to the number 7 shirt which had previously been worn by team legends such as George Best, Eric Cantona and David Beckham. "After I joined, the manager asked me what number I'd like. I said 28. But Ferguson said 'No, you're going to have number 7' and the famous shirt was an extra source of motivation. I was forced to live up to such an honour."

Ronaldo made his team debut as a 60th-minute substitute in a 4-0 home victory over Bolton Wanderers, and scored United's 1000th Premier League goal in October 2005 in a 4-1 defeat to Middlesbrough. He scored his 50th career United goal against city rivals Manchester City FC as the Reds' claimed their first Premier League title in four years in 2006-07. Despite rumours circulating in March 2007 that Real Madrid were willing to pay an unprecedented €80 million (£54 million) for Ronaldo, he signed a five-year, £120,000-a-week extension with United, making him the highest-paid player in team history. He amassed a host of personal awards for the season including the PFA Players' Player of the Year and PFA Young Player of the Year awards, joining Andy Gray (in 1977) as the only players to receive this honour.

In the last game of the season 2007-08, the Champions League final against league rivals Chelsea, Ronaldo scored the opening goal after 26 minutes, which was negated by a

Chelsea equaliser in the 45th minute as the match ended 1-1 after extra time. His misfire in the penalty shootout put Chelsea in a position to win the trophy but John Terry shot wide right after slipping on the pitch surface and United emerged victorious 6-5 on penalties. Ronaldo was named Man of the Match and wrapped up the campaign with a career-high 42 goals in all competitions, falling just four short of Denis Law's team-record mark of 46 in the 1963-64 season.

The international stage has also been blessed with his skills and goals. He was called up for Euro 2004, scoring in a 2-1 group stage loss to eventual champions Greece and in a 2-1 semi-final win over the Netherlands. He was named in the team of the tournament despite finishing with only two goals. In the 2006 World Cup, he was the second-highest scorer in the European qualifiers with seven goals, and scored his first and only World Cup goal against Iran with a penalty. During a quarter-final match against England, Ronaldo's United team-mate Wayne Rooney was sent off for stomping on Portugal defender Ricardo Carvalho. The English media speculated that Ronaldo had influenced referee Horacio Elizondo's decision by aggressively complaining about the infraction. He was also seen in replays winking at the Portuguese bench following Rooney's dismissal. After the match, Ronaldo insisted that Rooney was a friend and that he was not pushing for him to be sent off. Rooney said, "I bear no ill feeling to Cristiano, but am disappointed that he chose to get involved. I suppose I do, though, have to remember that on that particular occasion we were not team-mates."

The rumour that he still wants to go to Real Madrid will not go away. At the start of the 2008-09 season he confirmed that he would stay at United for at least another year. His mother would like him to play for Real Madrid one day, and even a multi-millionaire sports superstar must do what his mum tells him!

▲ Cristiano Ronaldo celebrates scoring his team's fifth goal against Stoke City, 2008.

▲ Wayne Rooney has been much compared to Michael Owen.

Rooney

Merseyside teenager Wayne Rooney has been compared with Paul Gascoigne for his precocious talents – but in reality his breakthrough to international fame was more similar to fellow Liverpool lad Michael Owen. Just as the previously little-known Owen starred in the 1998 World Cup, Rooney took the 2004 European Championships in Portugal by the scruff of the neck, scoring four goals in the group stages and, before he broke a bone in his foot in the quarter-final against the home nation, looked to be in the running for player of the tournament honours.

He'd graduated to the Everton first team in 2002 aged just 15 and was initially shielded from the limelight by manager David Moyes. But goals such as his 30-yard winner against Arsenal (and England goalkeeper David Seaman) making him the youngest goalscorer in the Premier League at the age of 16 years and 360 days inevitably bought him to the attention of England manager Sven Goran Eriksson.

Four months later he was awarded his first cap for England, becoming the youngest player to represent his country at 17 years 111 days (since surpassed by Theo Walcott). One hundred and six days later, against Macedonia in a European Championship qualifier, he became the youngest player to score for his country.

His first 15 England games brought seven goals, compared with Owen's five, but it was his Euro 2004 brace against Croatia, following a previous pair against Switzerland, that marked him down as a world-class star – especially since the Croats had publicly targeted him for rough treatment. Rooney's volatile

◀ Wayne Rooney in action.

temperament was undoubtedly at odds with Owen's ice-cold demeanour on the pitch, but England team-mate Rio Ferdinand proclaimed him "more streetwise than Michael was six years ago". That down-to-earth quality would be severely tested after the start of the 2004-05 season when he moved along the East Lancs Road to Old Trafford, Manchester. United's eagerness to snap him up for £22 million was undiminished by the broken foot sustained in the European Championships.

The fee (a world record for a teenager) was the second highest for an exclusively British deal, with only new team-mate Rio Ferdinand commanding a bigger figure. He has gone some way to repaying Sir Alex Ferguson's belief in him by helping the club to win two Premier League titles, a League Cup and the Champions League in 2008 – the year in which he also married his childhood sweetheart Coleen McLoughlin.

Scotland

▶ George Burley with his assistant coach Terry Butcher.

▶▶ The Tartan Army continue to sing despite the scoreline during the Euro 2008 qualifier against Italy.

Scottish football has a long and varied history. From the early days, when Irish immigrants helped to build a stadium for Celtic Football Club at Parkhead, Glasgow, to the present day, with Celtic and Rangers dominant in the domestic league, the game has always held a fascination for the Scots. In recent decades the dominance of Rangers and Celtic has meant that other sides can barely get a look-in, and this has caused problems for those other clubs – and for the league itself. Many of the smaller clubs have faced, or are facing, bankruptcy, and from time to time the call comes for the big two to join the English Premier League.

Rangers and Celtic would indeed bring extra spice to the English league, but their absence from Scottish football might actually cause more difficulties for the rest of Scotland as some very large "gates" would be lost. The Scottish game has not always been dominated by the Old Firm. Both Heart of Midlothian and Hibernian, the Edinburgh equivalent of Glasgow's big two, have won the Scottish league title on several occasions, Aberdeen winning it as recently as 1980, and then again in 1984 and 1985. It remains to be seen whether or not any side will come along to rival the Glasgow clubs in the future.

On the international front, Scotland has often flattered to deceive. Many Scots blame the fact that, in the past, some of their best players plied their trade in England, and never seemed to play as well when they returned home for international appearances. Today, Rangers and Celtic employ large numbers of foreign players and this also probably damages the prospects for up-and-coming Scottish footballers. It

seems likely that international success will continue to evade Scotland for the foreseeable future particularly after their most successful manager Alex McLeish (seven wins out of 10 matches) resigned after the country's narrow failure to qualify for Euro 2008 to go and manage Birmingham City. The weight of expectation from the Tartan Army has passed to new manager George Burley who did not win too many friends by appointing staunch Englishman Terry Butcher as his assistant.

Shearer

▼ Alan Shearer bidding farewell at his testimonial.

Although Alan was born in Newcastle he began his career with Southampton, one of the clubs furthest away from his hometown! He joined the Saints as a trainee and was upgraded to the professional ranks in April 1988, making an explosive start to his career and going on to become the youngest player to score a hat-trick in the (old) First Division. After 118 league appearances for Southampton and having netted 23 goals he was sold to Blackburn Rovers for £3.6 million in July 1992, and it was at Ewood Park that he developed into a highly polished and accomplished striker.

He became the first player to net as many as 30 goals in three consecutive seasons since Jimmy Greaves in the 1960s, the first player to net as many as 100 goals in the Premier League, and helped Blackburn Rovers to the Premier League title in 1995. His form at club level was repeated at international level, finishing the 1996 European Championship finals as the top scorer with five goals to his credit.

Shortly after helping England reach the semi-finals of the European Championship he was sold to Newcastle, costing his hometown club a British record fee of £15 million. Although he announced his retirement from international football after the 2000 European Championships, he spent the remainder of his career with the club.

While he would never emulate the success of his time at Blackburn Rovers, Shearer won runners-up medals in the Premier League and FA Cup with Newcastle, and a second PFA Player of the Year award.

He is both Newcastle's and the Premier League's record goalscorer. Following his retirement from football, Shearer has been linked with managerial positions at his former clubs particularly at Newcastle when Keegan walked out in September 2008; however, he continues to bide his time while the club is in turmoil and enjoys a relatively stress-free life working in the media with the BBC.

Shilton

▲ Shilton takes a break during the 1990 World Cup.

Peter Leslie Shilton was born in Leicester on 18th September 1949. He signed for his hometown club in September 1966 and made his debut shortly afterwards, displacing the great Gordon Banks. Indeed, it was the potential of Peter Shilton that enabled Leicester to offload Banks to Stoke City. He picked up a runners-up medal in the FA Cup with Leicester in 1969 (his only appearance in the FA Cup final) before his transfer to Stoke, ironically following Banks, in November 1974.

After three years he was signed by Nottingham Forest and formed the backbone of the side that won the League Championship and two European Cups in successive seasons as well as the League Cup in 1979 and a runners-up medal the following year.

After 202 appearances for Forest he moved to Southampton and made a further 188 appearances for the Saints before joining Derby County and racking up another 175 appearances. First capped for England in 1971 against East Germany, he won a total of 125 caps to become England's most capped player, a figure that might have been even greater were it not for Ron Greenwood playing Shilton and Clemence in alternate games since he couldn't decide who was the better keeper.

He bowed out of international football after the 1990 World Cup finals and joined Plymouth as player-manager, although he went into semi-retirement as a player in order to concentrate on management. When he lost his job in 1995 he resumed his playing career, going on to become the first player to appear in 1000 league matches, a figure achieved whilst playing for Leyton Orient.

Television

▶ Ian Hutchinson was Chelsea's star in the 1970s.

▶▶ Rory Delap excelling at one of his long low throw-ins.

▼ Setanta Sports, a recent arrival in the world of football viewing.

With wall-to-wall matches, starting at 12 noon and sometimes not ending until 10pm, it is hard to recall the time when television and football did not go hand in hand. Indeed, television and football did not develop a proper relationship until somewhat late in the day.

The first FA Cup final to be broadcast live was the 1938 clash between Preston North End and Huddersfield Town, but there were more people in attendance at the match – 100,000 – than saw the game on television, there being less than 10,000 sets in the country. Even fewer had seen some of the earlier attempts at broadcasting live matches, a 1936 encounter between Arsenal and Everton probably the first.

It was highlights programme *Match of the Day* that fuelled real interest in the game, the first programme going out on BBC2 in August 1964 with highlights of Liverpool's home win over Arsenal. Viewing figures of 75,000 were only slightly higher than those who attended the match, but the programme soon became a ratings winner, prompting the rival independent network to launch their own highlights programme.

It was to take until 1983 before regular live football made its appearance on the programme schedule, with Spurs' home match against Nottingham Forest switched to a Sunday in October with little or no impact on the gate. But at the start of the 1985-86 season the football authorities were unable to conclude a deal with TV and so the screens remained blank.

The arrival of Sky changed the game; it could be said that the Premier League came into being because of television. The recent arrival of Setanta who share both Premier League and England matches with Sky and the terrestrial channels is another indication that TV football is here to stay and will dominate even more.

Throw-ins

It was the Sheffield FA (under whose rules the Sheffield side, the world's oldest football club having been formed in 1857, play) that first introduced the notion of a throw-in to restart the match after it had gone over the touchline. The FA's rules had dictated a kick-in, similar to a goal kick, but having observed the Sheffield rules subsequently adopted a similar ruling.

To begin with, there were no restrictions on the throw-in; players threw the ball one-handed, similar to a goalkeeper's throw-out and achieved similar distance. In time, the more accepted two-hand, both feet on the ground ruling was adopted.

There are some players to whom the two-handed throw is seen as little or no disadvantage. One of the most comical moments of the 2002-03 season was the sight of Aston Villa goalkeeper Peter Enckelman misjudging a throw-in from one of his defenders and missing the ball as it headed towards his goal. Although Enckelman did not touch the ball (it is not possible to score direct from a throw-in), the referee believed he did, judging by his desperate attempts to retrieve it, and the goal stood.

Chelsea in the 1970s had a long-throw specialist in Ian Hutchinson with his windmill-like action, while the longest modern-day exponent is Stoke City's Rory Delap who manages to keep the trajectory relatively low causing havoc amongst defenders as the ball shoots in to the penalty area.

Although FIFA tried out a replacement kick in a junior tournament in 1993, these plans were subsequently scrapped. Given the histrionics we see at corners, perhaps FIFA are right to leave the throw-in well alone!

Transfers

▶ Robinho who holds the record for the highest British transfer fee.

Almost as soon as Football began to get itself organised, clubs have offered ever-increasing sums in order to secure the services of one player or another. It was in 1908 that the first attempt to control the transfer fee was made, a ceiling of £350 being set by the Football Association as a result of Alf Common becoming the first player to be transferred between clubs for £1,000. This soon proved to be unworkable, with clubs throwing in reserve players and claiming that they were worth the full £350, so the ceiling was abandoned three months later.

Thereafter the transfer limit grew and grew. The first five-figure fee was paid by Arsenal to Bolton Wanderers in 1928 for David Jack and was for £10,890, £10,340 or £10,670 depending on sources. Just short of 30 years later John Charles was the first player to be transferred for more than £50,000, Italian side Juventus paying £65,000 for his signature in June 1957. It was another three years before one English club paid another more than £50,000, Denis Law costing Manchester City this sum.

A little over a year later, Law's value had rocketed, at least as far as Torino were concerned, paying £100,000 to take the striker to Italy in July 1961. Law had 12 months in Italy before he returned home, to Manchester United, for £115,000 to become the first player bought by an English club for in excess of £100,000 (Jimmy Greaves might have been the first some months earlier, but Bill Nicholson deliberately held out for a transfer fee of £99,999 in order to prevent Greaves being labelled the first £100,000 player when moving from AC Milan to Spurs).

The next two milestones were reached within weeks of each other. In June 1977 Kevin Keegan was transferred from Liverpool to Hamburg for £500,000, and in January 1979 David Mills became the first player to switch between English clubs for this sum when West Bromwich Albion paid Middlesbrough £510,000 for his services. Five weeks later, Nottingham Forest paid Birmingham City £975,000 for Trevor Francis, VAT and the player's percentage taking the final bill to £1,150,000.

At present the British record is the

£32.5 million Manchester City paid Real Madrid for Robinho at the end of August 2008, but this is still only the fifth highest fee paid in the world, Real Madrid paying Juventus £45.6 million for Zinedine Zidane, only a year after they had paid Barcelona £37.4 million for Luis Figo.

UEFA

▼ Manchester United manager Alex Ferguson holds the trophy after beating Chelsea in the UEFA Champions League Cup final, 2008.

It was 50 years after the formation of FIFA that Europe, always the motivating force, felt compelled to organise the Union of European Football Associations (UEFA) in 1954. To begin with, UEFA had no intention of organising competitions; this was to be almost imposed upon them.

The success of the European Champions' Clubs Cup (the name "European Cup" was to have been used for a national competition) prompted the launch of a similar competition for national cup winners, the European Cup Winners' Cup. Although there was a third competition, the Inter Cities Fairs Cup, this was never organised by UEFA and is not recognised by them as an official competition! That all changed in 1971 with the creation of the UEFA Cup.

Today UEFA, which has 53 members, organises 15 competitions, nine for national representative sides and six for clubs, which range from the European Championships and European Champions League through to a continental championship for five-a-side football, taking in a women's competition along the way.

When formed, UEFA had 25 national association members; subsequent political changes in Eastern Europe have more than doubled that number. More importantly, interest in its competitions, particularly the European Championships, has increased ten-fold. Former French international player Michel Platini is currently its president.

United

Manchester United was founded in 1878, when the club was known as Newton Heath. During the early years of the 20th century, United largely played second fiddle to Manchester City. This was also the case in the 1930s, when City spent every season except the last in the top division, while United were mainly a Second Division side. In 1934, United finished 21st in the old Second Division, and only narrowly avoided relegation to Division Three (North) while, at the end of that same season, City achieved 5th place in Division One.

Everything was to change after the Second World War. United gradually came to reign supreme in Manchester and, in 1952, they won their first League Championship for 41 years. They won it twice more during the 1950s, and twice during the 1960s. After that however, the top spot was to elude them until 1993 when they were champions of the newly formed Premier League. Between 1993 and 2008 they won the Premier League title no fewer than 10 times. United had won the European

▼ David Sadler beats George Best to hoist the European Cup aloft, 1968.

▲ Fergie's Fledglings now rival the Busby Babes as the greatest United team ever.

Cup in 1968, when they beat Benfica 4-1 (after extra time) at Wembley, and they were to win the European Championship again in 1999 and 2008 – each time also winning the domestic league title in the same year. They have also won the FA Cup 11 times.

Manchester United's record is of course an excellent one. United are arguably the best known club side on earth and they have supporters' clubs all over the globe. Whilst their star players have grabbed the headlines – Best, Law, Charlton, Giggs, Cantona and Ronaldo – it is the managers who have also helped bring home the trophies. Following in the tradition of Sir Matt Busby, Sir Alex Ferguson has been manager since November 1986 in which time United have won 20 major trophies. His importance to the club is incalculable and it has become a favourite game of fans to guess his successor when he eventually does retire. A number of former players including Mark Hughes and Roy Keane are amongst the favourites. Who would also bet against current club captain Gary Neville who was born in Greater Manchester?

▲ Uruguay in early World Cup action, scoring against Argentina in the 1930 final.

Uruguay

Winston Churchill once described Russia as "a riddle wrapped in a mystery inside an enigma." He could just so readily have been describing Uruguay, a country whose abilities as a footballing nation vary between the sublime and the ridiculous.

The first country to win the World Cup, their exploits for the 50 or so years have seen them leading disciples of the cynical football of the 1960s through to a talented side in keeping with their South American heritage.

Uruguay first emerged as a world power towards the end of the 1920s when they won the gold for football at the 1928 Olympics in Amsterdam. The success of the tournament prompted FIFA to finally institute a World Cup competition, to be held in Uruguay in 1930. Organised on a straight knock-out basis, Uruguay made it to the final to play their closest neighbours and rivals Argentina and won 4-2. However, as most of the major European footballing

▲ The team of Uruguay, 2008.

nations had not bothered to make the journey to South America, Uruguay refused to journey to Italy to defend the Jules Rimet trophy in 1934! They stayed away again in 1938, returning to the fold in 1950 in Brazil.

Required to play only one qualifying match, in which they beat Bolivia 8-0, Uruguay took their place in the final pool along with Brazil, Sweden and Spain. A draw against Spain and one-goal victory over Sweden preceded a game (effectively the final) against a Brazilian side that had won both of their matches against Spain and Sweden. It meant Brazil needed only a draw to be crowned world champions, whilst Uruguay would have to quieten 200,000 Brazilians squeezed into the Maracana Stadium. After a goalless first half, Brazil took the lead and seemingly the title, but goals from Schiaffino and Ghiggia took the trophy to Montevideo for the second and so far last time.

Semi-finalists in Switzerland in 1954 (where they were beaten by the Mighty Magyars), Uruguay next made an impact, albeit for all the wrong reasons, in 1966. Qualifiers, along with England from Group 1, Uruguay were pitted against the West Germans in the quarter-final. Their battle was virtually a mirror image of the European/South American clash going on between England and Argentina at Wembley; Uruguay hit the bar, had a good penalty claim turned down and lost their heads, two men and four goals in a heated second half.

Better behaved and better rewarded in 1970, they made it as far as the semi-final before bowing out to the Brazilians. That proved to be their last meaningful contribution to the World Cup finals, for although they have qualified four further times (once via the play-offs against Australia) they have not progressed beyond the early rounds.

Van Basten

▲ Ajax coach Marco van Basten, 2008.

Having helped first club Ajax win the Dutch league in his first full season, 1982-83, Marco van Basten (born 31st October 1964 in Utrecht, Holland) made his big breakthrough in the 1983-84 campaign when he scored 28 goals in 26 games. Having made 143 league appearances and scored 128 times for Ajax, he signed for AC Milan in 1987-88 but was immediately afflicted by an ankle injury.

The 1988 European Championships gave him the chance to make an improbably swift comeback, setting up Holland's first goal against Russia in the final and scoring the second with a memorable volley from an impossible angle. He finished the competition's top scorer with five and finished a supposedly dead season World Footballer of the Year.

In-between injuries, the player scored an incredible 90 goals in 147 Serie A games (including 25 in 1991-92, a personal record) and had a better than 90 per cent conversion record at penalties, a statistic that made his European Championship failure against Peter Schmeichel the more inexplicable.

Van Basten, who retired through injury in 1995, was selected as the best player in Europe in 1988, 1989 and 1992. He was appointed national manager after Euro 2004, and in his four years in charge the Dutch side flattered to deceive particularly at the European Championships in 2008 where they looked hot favourites to win. He returned to his first club as manager after the Championships.

Villa

▲ The two new stars in the Villa team, Gabriel Agbonlahor and Ashley Young.

▶ Ryan Giggs celebrates with team-mates, Carl Fletcher and Simon Davies, after Giggs scored a goal from a free kick, 2005.

Aston Villa, Birmingham's senior club by the matter of a single year, have been one of English football's biggest for as long as the game has been played, though in recent decades they have under-achieved in relation to their stalwart support. Their status has also been enhanced by Villa Park, a ground regularly used to stage FA Cup semi-finals and, in 1996, European Championship games.

Villa became only the second club ever to win the League and Cup Double in 1897, thanks to the goals of John Campbell and George Wheldon. More recently, they won the European Cup in 1982 under assistant manager Tony Barton (Ron Saunders having resigned earlier in the season) to signal a brief return to the heady heights of those early glory days.

Their other highlight of recent years came in 1990 when Graham Taylor took them to second in the top flight, having obtained promotion the previous season, but he was poached to become England manager. The series of men who replaced him – Ron Atkinson, John Gregory, Josef Venglos and David O'Leary among them – proved inadequate for the task, and it wasn't until the appointment of Martin O'Neill in the summer of 2006 that the club threatened to break in to the top four in the Premier League. Around the same time chairman and single biggest shareholder (approximately 38 per cent), Doug Ellis finally decided to sell his stake in Aston Villa to American businessman Randy Lerner, the owner of NFL franchise the Cleveland Browns. The mood of optimism at Villa Park has been boosted by a crop of talented young players including Ashley Young and Gabriel Agbonlahor although club captain Gareth Barry still threatens to rock the boat with his desired move to Liverpool.

Wales

Traditionally, Welsh soccer has always been in the shadow of rugby football and it used to be seen by many Welshmen as a second-class sport. The decline in the fortunes of Welsh rugby did, however, coincide to an extent with increasing interest in the round-ball game and, over the past 50 years or so, the Principality has produced some excellent players.

The most notable of these was inside forward Ivor Allchurch. Born in Swansea, he made 330 league appearances for his hometown club, before moving on to Newcastle and then Cardiff. He finished his career back in Swansea in 1968, but in-between times he played 68 times for Wales. Ivor was very quick, had excellent ball control, and was a prolific goalscorer – netting 251 times in a total of 682 league appearances. His

▲ John Toshack, the current manager of Wales.

brother Len, an outside-right, was also a very good footballer and he won 11 Welsh caps. Centre-half Mel Nurse was another Swansea boy who made the big time with Swansea, Middlesbrough and Swindon, and played for Wales on 12 occasions.

More recently, Wales has produced the likes of Ian Rush and Ryan Giggs. Superb striker Rush made 658 appearances for Liverpool, scoring 346 goals in his two spells with the club. He moved briefly to Juventus, but whilst at Anfield he played 73 times for his country. Manchester United's Ryan Giggs played more than 60 times for his country but, under the influence of manager Sir Alex Ferguson, always seemed to put his club first and should have really challenged Neville Southall as the country's most capped player.

On the international front, Wales have recorded comparatively little success, although recent performances have often been a lot better than many outside the Principality expected. The most notable achievement came in the 1958 World Cup when, against all the odds, Wales progressed to the last eight. Brazil were their quarter-final opponents and, had it not been for a rather accomplished 17-year-old player called Pelé, who scored the game's only goal, they might well have progressed further. Wales will hope to do better in the 2010 World Cup qualifying campaign under the returning John Toshack, who succeeded Hughes as national coach in November 2004.

Wembley

The new Wembley Stadium was opened in March 2007 at a cost of £737 million with a capacity of 90,000. Whilst the stadium is a dream venue most football fans think that the owners missed a trick by not having more seats so that it really is the biggest and the best. The eye-catching arch – at 315m, the longest single-span roof structure in the world – has the same iconic status as the old Empire Stadium's twin towers but at least the old stadium could hold more than 100,000 spectators. Indeed around a quarter of a million turned up for its first big game, the 1923 FA Cup final, to watch Bolton Wanderers play West Ham, and they almost took part in a national disaster. In the event, this was avoided by allowing large numbers of people onto the pitch and controlling them with an army of mounted policemen. The official attendance figure was 126,047, but it's certain that the real figure was much higher.

Wembley hosted the Olympic Games

▲ An aerial view of Wembley during the 1923 Cup final, showing the twin towers on the right.

◀ The new and controversial Wembley takes shape with its new tubular arch.

▲ Wembley with its eye catching arch.

in 1948, and the World Cup final of 1966. However, after 1923, its main claim to fame was as the venue for the FA Cup final. Every club wanted to "get to Wembley" and the old place staged the final until the end of the century. By then it was in sore need of reconstruction, and eventually the decision was taken to pull it down and start all over again. The rebuilding of Wembley was a long and tortuous process and while the stadium was closed the FA Cup final and other big matches were played at the Millennium Stadium, Cardiff, for five years from 2002. Since re-opening, the stadium also now plays host to the FA Cup semi-finals as well as the Football League play-off finals and England's home internationals.

World Cup

It was Jules Rimet, the president of the World Football Federation, who started it all. Aided by a small committee, he organised the first tournament which took place in Uruguay in 1930. Only a handful of European countries took part and the home nation won the tournament, beating Argentina 4-2 in the final. It was a relatively small beginning but Monsieur Rimet had a vision. He believed that "Soccer could reinforce the ideals of a permanent and real peace" and, although he may have got this a little wrong, his tournament was to take off in a very big way.

In the 18 tournaments held, only seven nations have won the title. Brazil is the most successful World Cup team, having won the tournament five times. The current World Champions, Italy, follows with four titles, while Germany holds three.

The other former champions are Uruguay and Argentina with two titles each, and England and France with one title each. The most recent World Cup finals were held in Germany, where Italy were crowned champions after beating France in the final. The next World Cup finals will be held in South Africa, from June 11th to July 11th 2010, and the 2014 finals will be held in Brazil.

England's only success came, as everyone knows, in 1966. Alf Ramsey had fashioned his team of "wingless wonders" and truly believed that the ultimate triumph was possible. At times it seemed unlikely, but a quarter-final victory over Argentina and a semi-final

▲ The current World Cup was adopted after three time winners Brazil were awarded the Jules Rimet trophy in perpetuity.

▲ Brazil currently hold the record of four World Cup wins.

win against Portugal meant that England reached the final. West Germany were to prove hard to beat, but Alf believed.

The Germans took the lead in the first half, but Geoff Hurst had levelled the score by the interval. Martin Peters made it 2-1 in the second period and, as the minutes ticked by, it seemed that it was all over – but then, following a free kick, West Germany scored again, just seconds from the end of normal time. The rest is, of course, history. Alf rallied his troops, and in extra time (and with the approval of a friendly Russian linesman) Geoff Hurst scored England's third. Hurst then completed his hat-trick and, at 4-2, it really was all over. We haven't done quite so well since.

X Marks The Spot

It was a scene repeated in households around the country; every Saturday afternoon, at 4.45pm, fathers and grandfathers would huddle around the radio or, if they were well off, the television set, and listen with great intent to the football results.

In households in Torquay, what mattered most was not the performance of their own hometown team, but had Hartlepool managed to gain a creditable draw at Chesterfield? Meanwhile, in Hartlepool, they were more concerned with whether Fulham had come from behind to rescue a point at Portsmouth.

Before the national lottery and with the possible exception of the premium bond, the only way to (legally) acquire an instant fortune was predicting scores via the football pools.

They had been launched in 1923 by John Moores and two friends, all telegraphists, who invested £50 each and printed 4000 football coupons, which they distributed outside Manchester United's ground one Saturday afternoon. Only 35 of these were returned, with stake money of £5, and £2 of this was paid out in winnings in that first week.

▲ All pools coupons had to be checked individually by hand in the pre-computerised era.

By the end of the season, the

▲ The rich but ultimately tragic figure of 1961 pools winner Viv Nicholson.

venture had incurred losses of £600, a phenomenal amount for the time, and two of the group decided to cut their losses and move onto something else. John Moores, who called his company Littlewoods Pools, carried on alone and by the time he was 35 had made himself a millionaire.

Along the way he attracted competition, Vernons started in 1925 and Zetters in 1933, but it has always been Littlewoods that promised the biggest jackpots and, at times, the larger-than-life characters that won them.

Unlike betting on horses or other sports, the football pools have always appeared complex. You are not trying to guess which team will beat another, but which matches will end in draws! The popularity of the football pools was such that at its height, more than a billion coupons would be entered each season, and each of these would have to be checked by hand.

There were one or two spectacular winners too, most notably the Nicholson family in 1961. Miner Keith Nicholson and his liquorice factory-worker wife Viv scooped a jackpot of £152,000 (equal to £3 million in today's money) and, when asked what they intended doing with the money, replied "Spend, spend, spend."

Keith was killed in a car crash on his way to meet his racehorse trainer four years later and Viv had soon lost not only her husband but most of his money.

The launch of the national lottery, which offered greater jackpots for even less work, slashed interest in the football pools overnight (in 2001 Littlewoods' income from the pools was £44 million; by comparison, Camelot's from the lottery was £4.98 billion).

Despite this, there are still two million people a week who play the football pools, still dreaming of winning the jackpot, still hoping Hartlepool get a draw at Chesterfield.

▲ Geoff Hurst hits England's third goal in extra time to break the 1966 World Cup final deadlock.

X-Tra Time

There is no record as to when extra time was first introduced as a way of trying to separate two sides who'd drawn a cup tie. We do know that in 1898 Sheffield United refused to play an extra half an hour in a replay of the Sheriff of London's Shield (a forerunner to the FA Charity Shield), but this was in protest at some of the referee's decisions.

A law establishing extra time was introduced by the FA Council in 1912, although initially this was purely for the final itself. It was not until 1920 that extra time was first used in the FA Cup final, when Aston Villa and Huddersfield Town had battled for 90 minutes without either side scoring a goal. The players were obviously unsure of the arrangements as they all shook hands and walked off! It was the referee

▶ French forward David Trezeguet jubilates after scoring the golden goal in extra time during the Euro-2000 final.

who pointed out that they had another half an hour to go, upon which they returned to the field, Kirton of Villa finally managing to break the deadlock.

There have been some famous passages of play in extra time none more so than the 1966 World Cup final between England and West Germany which gave England two goals, one contentious, the other clear-cut, that are forever etched in the memory.

The advent of penalty shootouts have taken away some of the urgency of extra time in knockout competitions with some teams playing for a draw and preferring to take their chances in the penalty lottery at the end of the match, for example, Greece in the European Championships of 2004!

Other methods have been tried to encourage a result in extra time including golden goals (sudden death) and silver goals (where the extra time was split into two 15-minute periods; if one team led after the first 15-minute period, the game ended). However, the International Football Association Board (IFAB) thought penalties a more entertaining and fairer bet and discontinued their use in 2004.

▲ The incomparable Lev Yashin in action.

Yashin

Soviet goalkeeper Lev Yashin, born in October 1929, cut an imposing figure in his all-black kit. Nicknamed the Octopus in celebration of his all-encompassing handling, he was a fixture on the international scene behind the red-shirted Russian defence from the mid 1950s to 1967. Yet it could have been so different; disillusioned by his inability to make the Dynamo Moscow first 11, he considered switching sports to ice hockey (where he also kept goal) in 1953. Happily, he was not lost to football and Dynamo would be his only team after he finally displaced Tiger Khomich for both club and, eventually, country.

Yashin created a record in achieving 78 international caps, winning the 1956 Olympics and the 1960 European Championship with his country as well as finishing third in the 1966 World Cup – the third finals in which he'd participated. Little wonder his country gave him its top honour, the Order of Lenin, in 1968, the year after he bowed out of international football.

An outstanding athlete, he possessed agility and anticipation paralleled by few other goalkeepers, and his shot-stopping was outstanding; it is claimed he kept 270 clean sheets and saved over 150 penalties during his career. He retired in 1971 at 41 years of age, a team of European stars playing an exhibition match in his honour at the Lenin Stadium.

As well as helping Dynamo to many League and Cup triumphs, Yashin won the 1963 European Player of the Year award – the only goalkeeper ever to have won that prize. He had a leg amputated in 1986, the legacy of a knee injury, and died in 1990. A statue was erected in his memory at Dinamo Central Stadium in Moscow.

You'll Never Walk Alone

When American Oscar Hammerstein II first read Ferenc Molnar's play *Liliom* and then penned some lyrics for his friend Richard Rogers' musical *Carousel*, which was based on that play, he could never have believed that his little song would one day become the anthem of Liverpool Football Club.

Local singer Gerry Marsden covered the song with his backing band the Pacemakers and topped the chart in 1963. It was adopted by the Kop who saw it as a heartfelt expression of triumph over disaster – something to fire up the passion in their players spurring them on to victory.

▼ The Anfield Kop, whose rendition of *You'll Never Walk Alone* has become internationally known.

When you attended a football match prior to the 1960s, you heard little or no singing. Most people stood on the terraces and came up with no more than an occasional insult (often referring to the doubtful parentage of the referee) an occasional witticism and, on a good day, a bit of half-hearted chanting. Basically, you cheered, clapped or moaned, according to the state of the game, and then you either went for a pint or, more likely, home to the wife for a nice cup of tea. Those were indeed the days.

Singing and chanting is now a part of football, and it serves a dual purpose. Popular culture dictates that everyone should be fond of popular music, although there is not much that is musical about some of the singing heard at Premier League grounds, and there can be little doubt that singing and chanting encourages the players in their endeavours. It's all about atmosphere, and it also helps the bonding process amongst supporters, assuming they need it.

Zidane

▲ Zidane was sent off for head-butting Italian defender Marco Materazzi during the World Cup 2006.

Zinedine Zidane started professional life with Cannes before deciding to go west to Bordeaux in 1992. At the beginning of his third season with Les Girondins he was given his international debut and promptly scored two brilliant goals in a 2-2 draw with the Czech Republic on his home turf in Bordeaux's Parc Lescure. Almost at once the French press began to compare him with the great Michel Platini.

By the summer of 1996 Zidane was national coach Aimé Jacquet's first-choice playmaker. He had enjoyed his best season yet for Bordeaux, helping the club to reach the final of the UEFA Cup with some breathtaking passing and spectacular goals.

At Euro '96 in England, he looked tired after a long, arduous season and failed to deliver the goods. But Italian giants Juventus had already agreed to pay Bordeaux £3.2 million for his services, and "Zizou" quickly recaptured his best form in the famous black and white stripes, helping Juve challenge strongly on both domestic and European fronts. His efforts in steering them to two Champions League finals were rewarded with the 1998 Footballer of the Year award – recognition too of his leadership in that year's World Cup.

A move to Real Madrid in 2001 for a world record £45.6 million fee rejuvenated his career, and Champions League victory in 2002 was just reward for his efforts. His career ended in controversy though when he was sent off in the 2006 World Cup finals against Italy after head-butting defender Materazzi who he claimed had insulted his mother and sister.

Zoff

▼ Captain and keeper Dino Zoff, in grey joins the World Cup celebrations, 1982.

Goalkeeper Dino Zoff (born in February 1942) found fame relatively late in life. After playing lower-division football for Udinese and Mantova a move to Napoli put him in the spotlight, but it was joining Juventus for a record fee for a keeper in 1972 that lit the touch paper. He would go on to notch five League and two Cup wins, as well as the UEFA Cup (1977) with Juve.

In the colours of his country Zoff would win the European Championship in 1968, having made his debut in the quarter-final against Bulgaria. He retained his place in the semi-final and final against Yugoslavia but didn't make the team for the 1970 World Cup finals.

Undeterred, Zoff captained Italy to World Cup victory in Spain in 1982 at the age of 40, having earlier created a world record for not conceding an international goal from September 1972 to June 1974, a total of 1,142 minutes.

He cut his managerial teeth in Rome with Lazio (where he signed Paul Gascoigne) before taking on the national team in December 1999. His attempt to match Franz Beckenbauer's record as the only man to captain and manage a European Championship-winning side was just 20 seconds from fruition before 2000 home nation France stole his thunder. Zoff briefly rejoined Lazio for a second managerial spell, replacing Sven Goran Eriksson. In 2005, he was named the coach of Fiorentina but after saving the team from relegation on the last day of the season, Zoff was released from his contract.

Zola

Gianfranco Zola was voted the greatest Chelsea player of all time by fans at the club following his retirement. They were therefore somewhat surprised when he became manager of rivals West Ham United in September 2008 – although many see it as a period of apprenticeship for the Chelsea manager's job!

Zola had joined Chelsea in November 1997. Born in Oliena, Sardinia on 5th July 1966, he had been the successor to the equally diminutive, and far less resilient, Diego Maradona at Napoli. Whilst in southern Italy Zola had won an Italian Championship medal, and he later picked up a UEFA Cup winner's medal with Parma. He had 26 Italian caps to his credit by the time he arrived at Stamford Bridge as a 31-year-old, but Gianfranco still had a great deal to offer.

Zola was a hard worker, read the game beautifully and showed tremendous vision as, in his first season at Chelsea, he helped his team to win both the European Cup Winners' Cup and the League Cup as well as the FA Cup in 1999-2000. At the age of 37, and having played in 266 games for Chelsea, scoring a total of 64 goals, he finally returned to his beloved island home in 2003. In 2006 he was appointed assistant coach of the Italian Under-21 side but had ambitions to be a Premier League manager which the Hammers (out of the claret and blue) allowed him to fulfil. He maintained his Chelsea connection though by stealing Steve Clarke from the club to act as his coach.

▲ Gianfranco Zola who replaced Alan Curbishley at West Ham.

Other books also available:

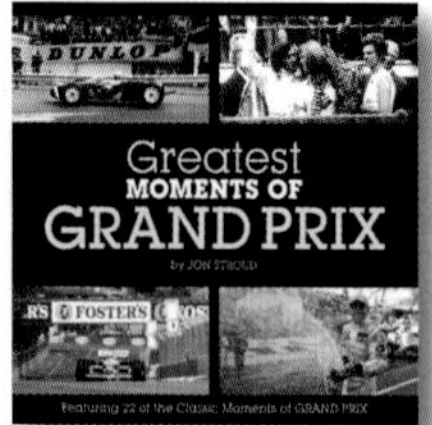

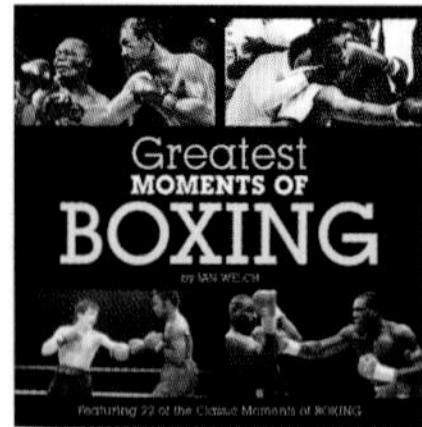

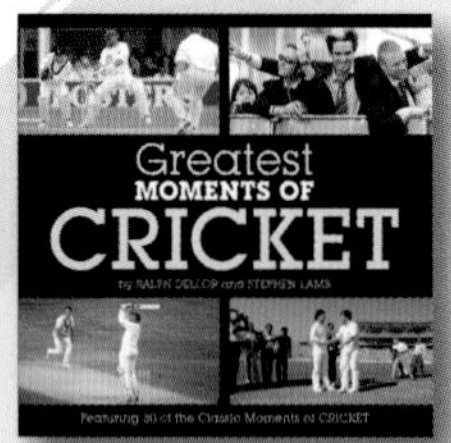

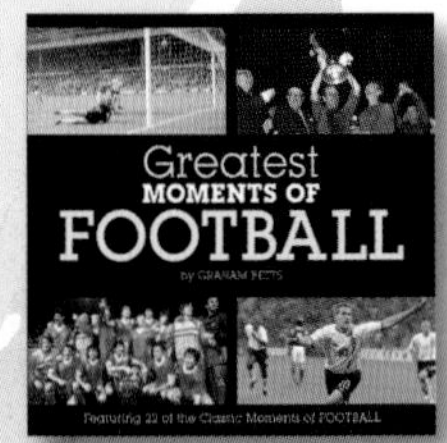

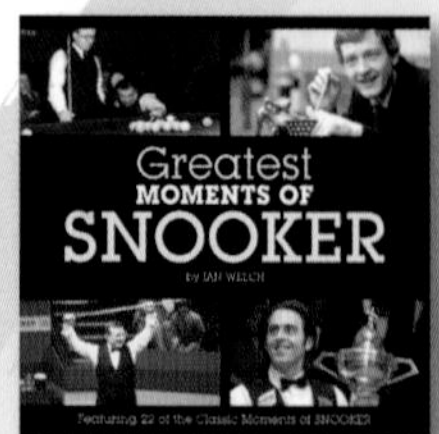

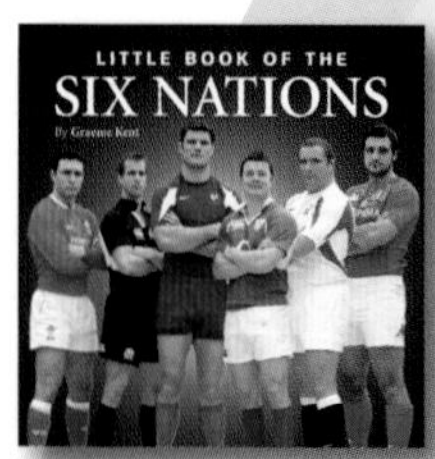

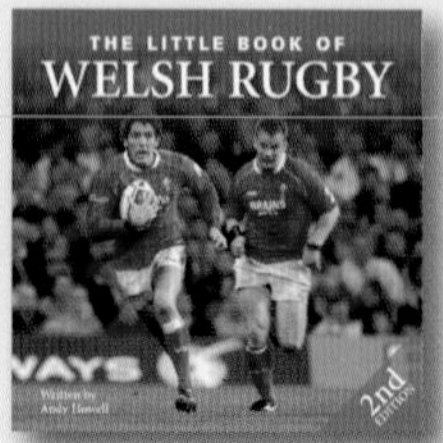

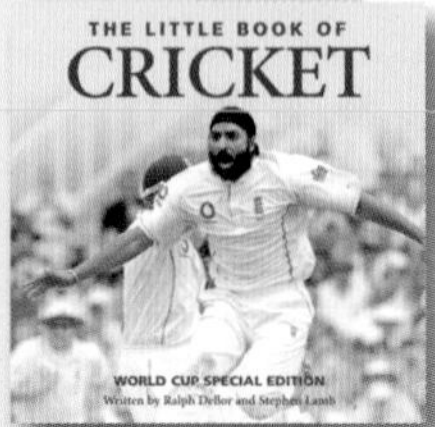

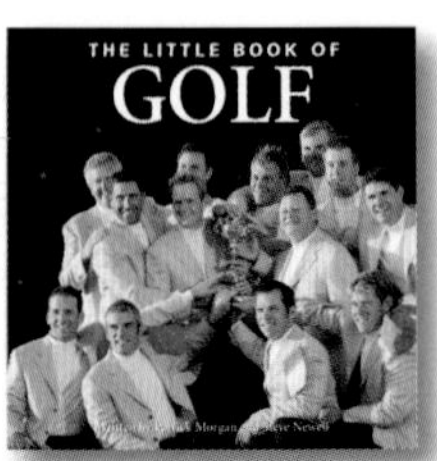

Available from all major stockists